# HOT RODs & CUSTOMs of the 1960s

Andy Southard, Jr.

Motorbooks International
Publishers & Wholesalers

## *Dedication*

To Mabel E. (Snyder) Southard
1906-1991

On Tuesday, December 9, 1941, my mother, Mabel Southard, joined the American Red Cross after the destruction at Pearl Harbor on December 7 and the start of World War II. Here she is in the Nassau County (NY) Chapter, American Red Cross, 1940 Ford station wagon. She was in the Motor Corp Division. I took this picture as Mother was ready to embark on an assignment. On the reverse side of this picture, in her handwriting, was written April 1947. The inset picture was taken in 1942 from her identification card.

First published in 1997 by Motorbooks International Publishers & Wholesalers, 729 Prospect Avenue, PO Box 1, Osceola, WI 54020-0001

© Andy Southard, Jr., 1997

All rights reserved. With the exception of quoting brief passages for the purposes of review no part of this publication may be reproduced without prior written permission from the Publisher

Motorbooks International is a certified trademark, registered with the United States Patent Office

The information in this book is true and complete to the best of our knowledge. All recommendations are made without any guarantee on the part of the author or Publisher, who also disclaim any liability incurred in connection with the use of this data or specific details

We recognize that some words, model names and designations, for example, mentioned herein are the property of the trademark holder. We use them for identification purposes only. This is not an official publication

Motorbooks International books are also available at discounts in bulk quantity for industrial or sales-promotional use. For details write to Special Sales Manager at the Publisher's address

Library of Congress Cataloging-in-Publication Data

Southard, Andy
  Hot rods & customs of the 1960's / Andy Southard, Jr.
    p. cm.
  Includes index.
  ISBN 0-7603-0329-0
  (pbk. : alk. paper)
  1. Hot rods—California—Pictorial works.
2. Automobiles—California—Pictorial works.
3. Automobiles—Customizing—California—Pictorial works.  I. Title.
TL236.3S67  1997
629.228'6'0979409046—dc21   97-4051

*On the front cover:* This roadster at the 1969 Oakland Roadster Show belonged to Anthony "Pancho" Martinez, who won first place. His 1929 Ford roadster had a 396-ci '67 Chevy engine with an Offenhauser manifold and Carter AFB carburetors. Tony custom built his outside exhausts with cut-outs channeling through Porter mufflers underneath. It had '65 Corvette disc brakes, a '67 Turbo Hydro transmission, and a '65 'Vette rear end. The paint is dark metallic blue with black upholstery.

*On the frontispiece:* This photo from June 1960 is looking out my front apartment window at my customized pearl white 1960 Ford Thunderbird. Silhouetted in the bay window are trophies from previous cars I had owned.

*On the title page:* In September 1965 the Bay Area Roadster Club held a "Stag" run, meaning it was just club members and no wives! As the event broke up, a lot of us stopped at Danny's Drive-In on Highway 1, an old-time "round" restaurant. In all, about six roadsters were parked, with the public getting a mini-car show.

*On the contents page:* Here I am in my '29 Ford roadster the day I photographed it for a feature in *Rod & Custom* in January 1965. When I acquired the roadster in 1961, it was black and had a Ford flathead. I installed a 327-ci Chevy engine and all the refinements, painted the roadster a blend of metallic maroon lacquer in my garage in Salinas, and pinstriped it in gold with white striped edges.

*On the back cover:* San Lorenzo, California, resident Don Brusseau, a charter member of the Bay Area Roadster Club, owned this 1925 T roadster pickup. Don painted the roadster Comet Ice Blue, and Banning of Gilroy, California, did the black Naugahyde upholstery. Don built his own chassis using 2 1/2-inch tubing. Power came from a 283-ci Chevy engine equipped with an Edelbrock manifold and Stromberg carbs. Spindles and front brakes were from a 1963 Ford Econoline van; rear brakes were from a '57 Ford station wagon. The roadster won the "People's Choice" award at the 1966 Roadster convention in Pismo Beach, California.

*On the back cover, inset:* I did a lot of pinstriping during the 1960s. In August of 1965, I had the pleasure of applying the white pinstripes to Dick Scritchfield's 1932 Ford roadster.

Edited by Michael Dapper
Designed by Amy Huberty

Printed in Hong Kong through World Print, Ltd.

# Contents

|  | **Acknowledgments** | **6** |
|---|---|---|
|  | **Preface** | **7** |
| Chapter 1 | **1960-1962** | **9** |
| Chapter 2 | **1963-1964** | **39** |
| Chapter 3 | **1965-1966** | **69** |
| Chapter 4 | **1967-1969** | **109** |
|  | **Index** | **128** |

*To Tom Chambliss —*
*Hot Rods and Customs of the '60s are really neat! Hope you enjoy my book!*
*Sincerely,*
*Andy Southard Jr.*
*6-20-97*

ANDY SOUTHARD, JR.
5 SAN JUAN DRIVE
SALINAS, CA 93901-3012
(408) 424-2149

# Acknowledgments

Following the overwhelming response to my first two Motorbooks International books, *Custom Cars of the 1950s* and *Hot Rods of the 1950s,* I was asked if I could do this book. The answer was yes, and I would like to thank Keith Mathiowetz of Motorbooks for all his support and believing in me—and for putting up with all my phone calls, inquiries, and talk about the 1960s for the past five months.

I do want to thank all the people who have enjoyed my first two books, especially those who have written and phoned, asking me to do more. It's you, the reader and enthusiast, who has made this possible. I have made so many good friends through my books.

Even though I am into the 1960s with this book, I must acknowledge some of my early buddies, as we all loved hot rods and customs: Willie Wilde and Johnny Clegg, both of Florida; Bill Acker of New York and Florida; and Ken Fleischmann and Bernard "Izzy" Davidson, both of New York, to name a few.

Again, much research has gone into this book, identifying cars and people. Assistance was given by: Greg Sharp, Rudy Perez, Mike Homen, Bob Pavao, Warren "Tut" Brown, Ron Yetter, Andy and Sue Brizio, John LaBelle, Rod Powell, Dave Marasco, Don Tognotti, Rick Perry, Tom Cutino, Larry Watson, Hershel "Junior" Conway, Jim Miraglia, Dick Jackson, Art Himsl, Jean Green, Joe Bailon, Neil Emory, Rich Pichette, George Barris, and John D'Agostino, all of California; Bob Kraus and Chuck Thuren, both of New York; Dick Scritchfield of Hawaii; Norm Grabowski of Arkansas; and Neal East of Colorado. And if I've forgotten anyone, you know who you are. Thank you.

# Preface

It is a pleasure to be able to do a third book for Motorbooks International. Five years ago, I never dreamed I would be going through my archives to show what transpired throughout the 1960s.

I took all of the pictures used here in the 1960s, and they were printed from my original negatives or my original 35-mm color slides.

Nearly all the pictures are of cars. The pictures are what I saw through my eyes and through my camera lens. At the time, they were taken strictly for my enjoyment and not for any historical record. This is a photographic record of my times and what I love to photograph. Please treat it as such. Enjoy my pictures and my personal experiences.

For those of you who haven't read my other two books, permit me to give you a short background of my early years. I was born and raised in Oceanside, Long Island, New York, and was an avid car buff, learning as a teen about hot rods and customs. I took a high school photography class and loved to take pictures of cars, which I processed myself and still do to this day. I later graduated from the New York Institute of Photography, spent time in Germany in the military, and after the service made numerous trips to California and back, some of them in the customized 1961 Ford Thunderbird you'll see in this book.

Nearly all of the pictures in this book were taken in California. When I searched through my archives, I found that I had approximately 2,808 slides covering the 1960s, so it was a difficult editing process to select only a few hundred slides for consideration for this book, and I have plenty more—maybe for future books!

While I was researching all my material, I saw the broad view of how the cars changed from the 1950s and on through the 1960s. I found paint schemes getting a little wilder, some of the early scallop jobs were more intense, cars were being flamed more, and besides the front flames, flames were licking back along the sides of the body. Even roofs were being flamed!

With the advent of the four-passenger Thunderbirds, cars were also getting the scalloped treatments. Corvettes were very popular, and were flamed, scalloped, or pearl-painted. Larry Watson of Southern California sure did his share of innovative paintings, and Dean Jeffries of Los Angeles was also doing plenty of flames, scalloping, and panel painting. You could give them credit for setting the paint themes of the 1960s.

Candy and pearl paints were very common. They were luscious colors of a pastel nature: tans, light blue, yellows, apricots, and colors that were blended and mixed as never before.

Cars in general, and customs in particular, were made lower to the ground, with customs lowered more than ever before, as you will see.

Customs were getting a little on the radical side and offset styling was coming into practice. Customizers such as Bill Cushenbery and Gene Winfield gave us some far-out show pieces. Upholstery was catching up, too. Beside Naugahyde, customizers integrated frieze materials, cloth, and pearl Naugahyde, which was more prevalent in the '60s, in contrast to just-plain-white, which had been the standard.

Pickup trucks, very popular in the 1950s, carried on into the 1960s, were seen in candy reds and pearls, and with wild interiors.

A lot of these cars were photographed at the shows I attended. Even though many of these cars were street-driven, they came from such a broad geographical area that I probably saw them only at the shows. A lot of the cars at the time were strictly show cars and were hardly driven, that I know for a fact! No disrespect meant, but that's the way it was!

Those that were driven probably ended up spending time at drive-in restaurants, which were still "the thing," even though a lot were going by the wayside. In Salinas, where I lived, I saw four of them fold up and go out of business.

Many of the pictures in this book are being published for the first time. They are from shows like the Oakland Roadster Show, Monterey Kar Kapades, San Jose Autorama, San Mateo Auto Show, Winternationals Car Show at the Great Western Exhibition grounds in Los Angeles, and the Hollywood Bowl parking lot, where the L.A. Roadster Club put on its first shows.

California had a lot of car clubs since the early days of racing on the dry lakes and the drag strips. You'll see some of the clubs' roadsters that were considered "Street Rods" at the time. They were driven quite often, especially on "Rod Runs," as they were known. As for myself, in the early 1960s, I was voted into the Bay Area Roadster Club (B.A.R.) and was an active member for 16 years. Membership qualifications in the B.A.R. were strict! A prospective member had to have a sponsor; a completed, running roadster; and to bring it to a few meetings for inspection so everybody could see your car. You had to participate in three runs and come to six of the monthly meetings. And finally, to be voted in—and get a unanimous "yes" vote to become a member. Needless to say, the rules have changed and are not as strict as when I was voted in.

I hope you will enjoy this book. Your thoughts and comments are welcomed.

*Andy Southard, Jr.*

# Chapter 1
# 1960-1962

It was an exciting time, the start of a new decade. Customizers still had easy access to the fabulous cars of the late-1950s, and a creative builder could always lay his hands on a choice vintage model from the '40s and beyond.

The production cars coming out of Detroit were still big and long, but fins were shrinking. An Oldsmobile "98" was the pace car for the Indianapolis 500 in 1960, followed by a Ford T-bird in '61, and a Studebaker Lark Daytona in '62. Jim Rathman won the '60 Indy 500, followed the next two years by a couple of American classics, as A.J. Foyt won in 1961 and Rodger Ward won in '62.

As far as current events of the era, the 1960 Summer Olympics were held in Rome, and a young Louisville boxer then known as Cassius Clay won the gold medal in the light heavyweight class. The '60 Winter Olympics were held in Squaw Valley, California, where the U.S. ice hockey team scored an upset that wouldn't be matched for another 20 years as it won the gold.

The big winners at the Oakland Roadster Show in the early 1960s were Chuck Krikorian, whose "Emperor," a '29 Ford roadster, won in 1960; Rich Guasco, the 1961 winner, also with a '29 Ford roadster; and George Barris, whose "Twister T," a '27 Ford roadster, won top honors in 1962.

The Los Angeles Roadster Club had its second-annual Roadster Show in October 1961 in the terraced parking lot of the Hollywood Bowl. It was early morning when I took this picture of Gary Heliker's '26 "T" roadster. Gary did all the work himself at his shop in Lawndale, California. The roadster sits on a '32 Ford frame with the body welded to the frame. The engine is a '55 Buick V-8 with three Stromberg 97 carbs, and it's backed up to a '39 Ford transmission with Zephyr gears and a rear end with a 3.78 ratio. Jade mist Naugahyde upholstery complements candy burgundy Metalflake paint. This roadster clocked 105 miles per hour in the quarter-mile. In the green shirt is movie actor Norm Grabowski.

This picture was taken in January 1960 at the San Jose Autorama. This is a 1959 T-Bird that was customized at Barris's shop in Lynwood, as the signature Barris crest is on the front quarter panel. It was lowered and painted candy red by Junior, and the hubcaps are customized. This is a good example of the candy red colors that were becoming quite popular in the early 1960s.

Bud Johnson of Los Angeles owned this '59 Ford Thunderbird, which is candy red and mildly customized. Eddie Martinez, the famous upholsterer, did the black-and-white pleated-and-rolled Naugahyde upholstery. The console and dash have custom pleats, and notice that the steering wheel and dash knobs are painted pearl white. With the hood partially up, you can see the three carburetors with chrome air cleaners. With the combination of the pearl interior and the candy red paint, this car really captures the flavor of the 1960s customizing.

Built originally in the mid-'50s by Rudy Heredia of Gilroy, California, this car was rebuilt by Buzz Sawyer of Watsonville, California, in the early 1960s. Buzz belonged to the Road Knights car club, and this picture was taken at the Monterey Kar Kapades in March 1960. The coupe is chopped and channeled, with bodywork and purple paint by M&M Muffler Shop in Watsonville. The gold-and-white Naugahyde upholstery with black rugs was done by Artcraft Upholstery of Watsonville, and the engine is a '51 Olds with a 4-inch stroke, a stock bore, a 270 Harmon & Collins cam, Jahns pistons, and '56 Oldsmobile heads. The intake manifold holds six Stromberg 97 carbs, and spark is supplied with a Scintilla Vertex magneto.

Jasper's 1950 Chevy coupe, which was built by Jasper Corpora of San Jose, a member of the Rod & Wheelers Club, was featured at the San Jose Autorama of 1960. Gene's Body Shop performed all the custom work. The quad headlights are deeply tunneled assemblies from a '57 Imperial, and the grille opening is shaped with round rod, while the grille bars consist of shaped-and-chromed 1-inch tube. Nerf bar-type bumpers protect the rolled pan and grille opening, and the hood is peaked down to the edge. Fender scoops were popular, as can be seen above the quad headlights. Dodge Lancer hubcaps with accessories are used on the wheels, and the paint is the popular rustic maroon. This Chevy is lowered by stepped "A" arms, and the frame has been "Z'd" in the rear.

During a January 1960 trip to Los Angeles, I went to see one of my heroes, Larry Watson, who I had only known casually for two years at the time. It was always fun visiting him. I shot a few pictures that day with Larry and his custom '59 Cadillac. I talked him into posing for me, simulating how he pinstripes, so as you can see, he didn't have any paint on his brush. Larry and I have become good friends through the years, and I see him often at the West Coast Kustoms events where we both participate. He even helped me identify some customs for this book.

A few cars in this book couldn't be identified despite my research. My complete magazine collection in the 1960s never had a feature on this outstanding coupe. This picture was taken at the February 1961 Oakland Roadster Show. Ron Price of San Jose owned this highly customized '34 Ford Coupe. The top was chopped 3 inches and the body was channeled over the frame 8 inches. Molded, modified fenders cover most of the rear wheels, and the front fenders are cut and have the style of a cycle fender. Other front-end modifications include the hood and nerf bars. The door and the trunk corners are rounded, and it has a completely chromed undercarriage. The custom upholstery was done by Sahagon. I have never seen this coupe again.

Rudy Torres from San Jose owned this 1959 Chevy Impala hardtop, which was photographed at the San Jose Autorama in January 1960. It was lowered to the ground, as most customs were, and typical of the average street custom, it sports a candy red paint job with Heinrich-style double-bordered scallops in gold. The ever-popular dummy spotlights are used, the grille consists of 12 chromed '53 Chevy grille pieces, and the hubcaps are customs with spinners. Trendy for the time was the red-and-white pleated upholstery, and the custom bodywork includes a smoothed hood and sunken radio antenna in the fender near the driver's door. This is a classic street custom from the early 1960s!

If memory serves me right, this is one of the last scallop jobs I did at H&H Auto Body in Rockville Centre, New York, where I did all my spray painting. The car was a black 1960 Pontiac Bonneville coupe. The mild scallop job was painted in candy red, with white pinstriping, as I am doing here, and I recall that the owner was pleased with my work. Most of my customers let me do what I wanted, for my styles and pinstriping were popular. This picture was taken in April 1960.

Don Tognotti of Sacramento showed his '32 Ford five-window coupe at the 1961 Oakland Roadster Show. It is chopped 3 inches and channeled over the frame 8 inches. The grille is chrome mesh and clear plastic tubes, and the car has a suicide-type front end with a tube axle and split front wishbones. The wheels are polished magnesium. The engine is a '51 Chrysler with '53 heads, a Weiand intake manifold with four Stromberg 97 carbs, and headers custom built by Brownie Muffler. The transmission is a '37 DeSoto with a beefed-up clutch. Named the "Avenger," it was painted in Aztec golden copper lacquer by Hugh Henderson of Sacramento, and the interior has black antique Naugahyde by Kustom Upholstery of Sacramento. Today, Don produces the Oakland Roadster Show.

This competition coupe originally belonged to Art Chrisman, who set and held a class record of 187 miles per hour at Bonneville. At the February 1961 Oakland Roadster Show, it was entered as the Barris-Geraghty rebuilt coupe, the XMSC (Experimental Speed Coupe). The body is a '31 Ford Model A that was chopped, channeled, sectioned, and it has a full bellypan for streamlining. The nose section is made from two '40 Ford hoods, and amber Plexiglas was used throughout, including the windshield and door windows. The paint is pearl white with diamond dust, accented with Kandy Tangerine. The doors are split and hinged on top to open like a Mercedes coupe. Its engine is a '58 Oldsmobile 460-ci engine with an Engle cam and Vertex magneto. The engine is coupled to a Halibrand quick-change rear by an "in-out dog box."

I have known Dennis Reinero for more than 30 years and little did I realize I would someday put his '56 Oldsmobile into a book. This picture was taken at the 1960 Sacramento Autorama, and it was unusual to have a four-door hardtop be a show-winning custom. The paint is pearl lavender and all the custom work was done by Winfield's Custom Shop in Modesto, California. The quad headlights have Lucas lights frenched in a round rod opening. The grille opening has expanded polished metal with 30 chrome bullets, which was popular at the time. The custom-chromed "lakes" pipes extend through the fender, and it has '57 Ford side trim. Taillights are frenched '59 Dodge lights. Today, Dennis owns a T-shirt factory in Santa Cruz, California.

To quote the show promoter, Al Slonaker: "Every year since 1949, the same time, same place, the granddaddy of all auto shows, the National Roadster Show! Come back Sunday night [February 26, 1961], see the awards ceremony, and watch the cars leave the building." It was always a thrill at Oakland to watch the awards ceremony and photograph the owners. That night I decided to stand on the exit ramp and photograph the roadsters leaving. This shot is extra special. It shows Mel Fernandes, the show manager (at right, in the white pants and shirt) leading Robert Curtin in his '26 T Roadster out of the building. Mel, who was a starter at the Calistoga races, got hit by a sprint car in 1974 and was killed.

Another outstanding street custom at the 1960 Sacramento Show was Bob Mayfield's '59 Chevy Impala. Custom work was done by Walker's Custom Shop of Bakersfield, and a custom grille was made from tubing, then chromed. The front and rear were lowered a total of 4 inches each. The side chrome trim was extended to run the full length of the car, and door handles were removed so the doors were opened electrically. Outside lakes pipes work in conjunction with outside exhausts, which run out the rear fenderwells toward the rear of the car. The interior is all-white roll-and-pleated pearl Naugahyde. Larry Watson did all the pearl painting and two-tone purple scallops and pinstriping.

The title of America's Most Beautiful Roadster at the 1961 Oakland show was won by PFC Rich Guasco of Pleasanton, California. Rich was in the service at the time, so his mother accepted the award in his absence, and it was an emotional moment. This high-boy is a '29 Ford roadster painted a wild Champagne Orchid Lacquer. Bodywork and paint were done by Joe Ortiz's Custom Shop. The wheels have been chromed and reversed, and the interior by Jerry Sahagon has solid pearl pleats, rolled edges, and rows of pearl buttons, all in Naugahyde. It has a '57 Chevy 301-ci engine with a Clay Smith cam, three 97 carbs, and custom outside chromed headers. This picture was taken at the Monterey Kar Kapades in March 1961.

"Madame FeFe." That's what John Buchan of Seattle, Washington, named his 1956 Chevy hardtop, shown here as it appeared at the March 1960 Oakland Roadster Show. John was one of four who competed in the Full Custom Hardtop Class. Wilson Customs takes credit for the bodywork. With a top that has been chopped 3 1/2 inches, dropped spindles, and a "C'd" frame, the car is lowered all around. Front and rear Studebaker pans house tubular grilles, and rear fender fins are cold rolled sheet metal, hammer welded, and molded to rear fender panels. The hood opens from its back edge, and the quad headlights are from a '59 Chrysler. The side trim is a combination of '58 Impala and '57 Buick trim, and the interior is Naugahyde and frieze. Power is supplied by a 339-ci Corvette engine.

Among the custom trends in the 1960s was the customizing of the popular pickups. Riley Collins of Chico, California, came up with this winner at the 1960 Oakland Roadster Show. His truck is a '55 Chevy Cameo Carrier that has fiberglass rear fenders and a bed that was factory stock. Custom taillights from an Edsel were frenched into the tailgate. The '56 Oldsmobile front bumper inset (hidden by a stanchion drum) has a handmade grille of chromed tube and mesh. Each side of the grille has '55 Buick bullets. The truck has chromed reversed rims, is lowered 4 inches, and sports a '57 Corvette engine backed by a Packard transmission. It is painted Mother of Pearl with candy red scallops, and the upholstery is white Naugahyde with red frieze inserts.

When I took this photo in August 1960, I was visiting Bill Cushenbery at his custom shop in Monterey. Notice his partial sign reads, "Custom Shop—Candy Painting." Another visitor was a friend of mine, Eddie Homen, and this is his customized '57 Chevy hardtop, lowered, with a nosed hood, and decked out with Plymouth hubcaps. The rolled-and-pleated interior was done by Manger of Castroville, and the candy green paint was mixed and sprayed by Ray Mathews of Monterey. Interestingly enough, the stock engine from this Chevy went into a '39 Chevy coupe, and a modified 283-ci Chevy from the '39 went into this '57 Chevy. My pearl white '60 Thunderbird sits in the background. Eddie passed away in July 1995, and he is missed.

### 1960s Oakland Roadster Show Winners

| | |
|---|---|
| 1960 | Chuck Krikorian, "Emperor," '29 Ford roadster |
| 1961 | Rich Guasco, '29 Ford roadster |
| 1962 | George Barris, "Twister T," '27 Ford roadster |
| 1963 | LeRoi "Tex" Smith, "XR-6," '27 Ford roadster |
| 1964 | Don Tognotti, '14 Ford roadster (oldest model to win) |
| 1965 | Carl Casper, "Ghost," custom fiberglass roadster |
| 1966 | Don Lokey, '27 Ford roadster |
| 1967 | Bob Reisner, "Invader," custom body roadster |
| 1968 (tie) | Bob Reisner, "Invader," (repeat winner) |
| | Joe Wilhelm, "Wild Dream," custom aluminum roadster |
| 1969 | Art & Mickey Himsl, "Alien," custom fiberglass roadster |
| 1970 | Andy Brizio, "Instant T," '23 Ford fiberglass roadster |

For the Monterey Kar Kapades in March 1960, Darryl Starbird from Wichita, Kansas, brought out his "Predicta" futuristic custom. It started out as a '56 Ford Thunderbird, and was completely totaled and gutted. Darryl completely hand-formed and rebuilt the body to become the dream car of the future he had in mind. It has a '57 Chrysler 354-ci engine with Hilborn fuel injection. The rear end is from a T-Bird, and the steering is a combination of Ford and Chrysler assemblies. It has center-mounted controls and "stick" steering. The grille is a collection of '59 Cadillac taillights coated white. The surrounding framework is 1 1/2-inch tubing, and the headlights are covered with Lucite panels. It has a clear plastic bubble top, white Naugahyde upholstery, and is painted a Satellite Blue Lacquer.

Another trip to Los Angeles in September of 1960 brought me to Barris Kustoms. It was always fun to see the cars that were around, some that I had never seen, like this one, a 1959 Buick hardtop. It's been lowered and has slight customizing to the taillights using '59 Cadillac taillight lenses. The hood was partially molded off, and it had some kind of cabinet-type handles as a grille piece. Popular at the time were the Lancer hubcaps and the Appleton spotlights. "Junior" Conway remembers that this Buick had minor bodywork and a taillight treatment. He painted it purple—and it was gone, never to be seen again.

Harry Costa's San Mateo Autorama of January 1961, had a special feature car, "The Beatnik Bandit," Ed Roth's latest creation. As the sign says, it appeared in the March 1961 issue of Rod & Custom and included drawings and parody by Joe "Guiseppe" Henning, "What Hath Roth Wrought?" A '50 Oldsmobile chassis was drastically shortened, and the body was made of fiberglass from a mold. Acry Plastics designed a clear plastic bubble and also supplied fiberglass materials. Single controls operate turning, braking, and the throttle. Eddie Martinez did the pearl white Naugahyde upholstery, and an Oldsmobile engine with a GMC Supercharger supplies the power. The grille is that of a late-model Ford. Roth painted, scalloped, and striped his creation himself.

In December of 1960, my friend Dick Mendonca and I visited customizer Joe Wilhelm at his shop on Chestnut Street in San Jose. As usual, the shop was filled up with parts and cars, one of which was "Mark Mist," a combination 1936/1940 Ford that was up on barrels and in pieces. The hood and doors were off, and the engine was out. The story goes that someone broke into the shop, took the engine out, and accidentally broke the windshield, which Wilhelm had quite a time replacing. Notice the hood perched up on the roadster to the left. Joe must have punched the louvers for a customer. I felt this picture was interesting enough to include since it depicts the lasting memory of the Wilhelm Custom Shop.

The first time I saw LeRoy Kemmerer's "Jade Idol" was at the January 1961 San Mateo Autorama. LeRoy is from Castro Valley, California, and he had Gene Winfield of Winfield's Custom Shop handle all the designing and metalwork. The car was originally a '56 Mercury and underwent a full 4-inch section job. The front features hand-rolled aluminum openings with frenched Lucas quad headlights with an adapted gear-type inner ring. The grille bars are rectangular with stainless steel inserts and rubber-tipped nerfs. The engine is a hopped-up '56 Mercury leading to a stick-shift Thunderbird transmission. With 15 trophies around the Mercury, it was very hard to get decent pictures of the car.

Robert Randall moved to Salinas from Kingsburg, California, in the early 1960s to attend college, and drove this lowered '59 Chevy Impala street custom. The coils were cut out of the front springs to lower the car, and lowering blocks were used at the rear. Body modifications were simple, as the emblem was removed, it was painted candy red, and received scalloped spotlights. It had a stock Chevrolet 283-ci engine, Dodge Lancer hubcaps, and gold rims.

Of the half-dozen cars that I have seen sectioned, one of the nicest was Lore Sharp's 1956 Buick Hardtop. Lore came all the way from Bremerton, Washington, to compete in the 1961 Oakland Roadster Show with this car, whose body was sectioned 4 inches by Lore's friend Gil Clifford. It has angled, frenched quad headlights and four frenched Packard taillights—even the rear license plate is frenched. Four-tube grille bars sit between a rolled upper and lower grille opening. Due to the sectioning, the hood had to be reshaped and it has rounded corners. The rear is done in similar fashion to the front end, featuring the rolled pans and grille bars. It has a modified Buick engine, and the candy red interior features bucket seats that swivel.

Joe Bailon of Hayward, California, did all the outstanding work on Dick Del Curto's 1950 Ford coupe, shown here at the San Jose Autorama in 1961. The unusual grille consists of a slender center bar with Oldsmobile turn signal lights floating in an oval opening with a fine-toothed section located below the bar. The headlights are frenched, and custom air scoops are found atop the fenders. The customizing treatment of the time is reflected by the fact that there are no door handles but there are ever-popular "lakes" pipes running underneath the door panel. One outstanding feature is the hand-formed, upswept, canted rear fender fins. Below the fins are custom taillights using reworked '56 Dodge units. The paint is candy gold, with candy red scallops and white pinstriping. The upholstery is red-and-white Naugahyde with gold beading.

Here's a view of two outstanding show cars at the Oakland Roadster Show in February 1961. On the left is Cushenbery's "El Matador" '40 Ford, and at the rear you can see the top of Bailon's "Scoopie Doo" '58 Chevy. To the right is Gordon Stefans's 1955 Plymouth hardtop. The front is highly customized with a floating bar grille, the bottom bumper grille from a '57 Dodge, and tubular grilles. The 1958 Buick parking lights are cupped in '55 Buick bumper tips. The interior and trunk are upholstered in white-and-orange Naugahyde, and the exterior paint is pearl white with orange sherbet, trimmed in gold. Western Wheel and Rim Company did the chromed reverse wheels.

Here is Tony Cardoza's customized '59 Chevy Impala. Fresh new restyling was performed by Cushenbery's Custom Shop, and the car appeared in the 1961 Monterey Kar Kapades. This front view shows the peaked hood, which is blended into the lowered, rolled pan. The quad headlights have '51 Mercury rings used to french and tunnel the lights. The grille is of chromed mesh with a custom floating bar and bullets on each end. Massive bodywork was done to achieve this new trend in styling.

Here is a three-quarter rear view of Tony Cardoza's '59 Chevy. The rear grille and body modifications follow the same theme as the front, with chromed mesh and custom floating bars, and Lucas taillights tunneled and frenched in extended rear fenders. Roof fins are styled to match fender fins, and the car is lowered with coil straps in front and a Z'd frame in the rear. The newly styled Royal Master tires are on chromed reverse wheels. Cushenbery calls this paint color "Shocked Red Lacquer." The doors, hood, and trunk operate electrically, and the interior moldings are chromed. Bill Manger did the pearl white Naugahyde upholstery and dashboard.

In the 1960s, when the dummy spotlights (bolt-on units) were becoming fashionable, I was kept busy scalloping and pinstriping. Patterns were taped on the spotlight, and insets were sprayed with color paint toner. Being transparent, the toner let the chrome base reflect whatever color was used, whether candy red, candy green, etc. Naturally, after the scallop was performed and painted, white striping enhanced the edges along with pinstripe designs. One customer at that time was Joe McDaniels of Salinas. It seems that every time he went to the movies and parked on a side street, his spotlights were stolen. He always came back and I did replacements for him, as shown in this August 1961 picture. Notice my "Pegger" Levi's and blue suede shoes, styles of the time!

This rear view of the Marquis shows the grille styling, which incorporated canted '59 Pontiac taillights. Four rows of chromed tubing fill the sculptured area, with mesh backing. The rear has '59 Buick fender fins incorporated into the original fenders' flared tips, and the rear fenderwells were opened and radiused. Notice the "V" flared styling on top of the fender tips. Power was supplied by a Thunderbird engine. This picture was taken at the San Mateo Autorama on January 6, 1962. Sadly, some years ago, Gene passed away, and since then, the Marquis has been owned by a few people, the most-recent owner being Bud Millard of Millbrae, California. At the time of this writing, the car is under restoration.

Gene Boucher of Monterey had the Cushenbery Custom Shop customize his '56 Ford hardtop. The two-and-a-half-year project set trends for the 1960s styling with a hood featuring an asymmetrical peak and concave sculpturing. The grille cavity houses horizontally mounted, chromed flat grille bars with a backing of chromed mesh. The quad headlights are frenched, with Lucas headlights and bullet-like bumpers canted inward from the reworked fenders. A new custom trend of the time is the concaves running from the front fender into the door. The main project for the "Marquis," as it was called, was the 6-inch section job. Manger did the Naugahyde upholstery, and the roof is padded and upholstered. Candy gold paint was applied by Don Mathews of Monterey.

Every time I see this photograph, I'm so glad I took it. It was not a planned picture, it was spontaneous, and I was just at the right place at the right time! It was taken March 4, 1962, the last day that the Bay Area Roadster Club participated at the Monterey Kar Kapades. After the show was over it was neat to see all the hot rods and customs leaving. As most of the Bay Area members left the show building, I was standing outside with camera in hand, and I turned on my strobe light, focused my camera, and took this picture. Shown here are (left-right): Ray Silva, Dave Marasco (sitting in the roadster), Paul Hannon (who owns the '29 roadster), Dick Mendonca, and Don Hentzell.

It was September of 1961 when I stood proudly beside my lowered 1961 Thunderbird. I wanted a black Thunderbird, and I knew exactly what I wanted to do when I got this one, which was to panel paint it in pearl white and pinstripe the edges in bright red! Panel painting was the fad then and I liked it. The only bodywork done was to take the Thunderbird emblem off the hood. When I paneled the Thunderbird, I put the pattern on with masking tape on Friday night, and Saturday I sanded and spray painted the pearl white at Kay's Body Shop in Salinas. The following weekend I pinstriped the edges in bright red and my street custom was finished!

I first saw Mel Taormino's '29 Ford roadster pickup in 1961 at the San Jose Autorama, in the secondary building at the San Jose Fairgrounds. The following year, Mel's roadster graduated to the main part of the building for the Autorama, which is where I first met and talked with Mel. The likable guy that he was (still is), he agreed on a date when I could photograph his roadster for a feature in *Rod & Custom* magazine, for which I was just starting to contribute. I took this picture on Mel's front lawn in February of 1962, and an article appeared in the May 1962 issue of *R&C*. It was the first feature I did for *Rod & Custom* which appeared on the cover.

Those of you who have read *Hot Rod*, *Rod & Custom*, and *Car Craft* magazines through the years have read about the upholsterers who did fabulous interiors. One such person you read about but never saw in pictures until now was Bill Manger. Here he is in action, shaping the foam seat in my '29 Ford roadster in 1962. Raised in Los Angeles, migrating to Watsonville, California, in the 1950s, Bill learned about upholstery by working in a shop, and in 1956 he opened his own shop in Castroville—and he's still there! He has upholstered many famous cars, such as Bill Cushenbery's "Silhouette," the "El Matador" '40 Ford, and the Ford Caravan "Astro."

Being a member of the Bay Area Roadsters, I participated in the Pismo Beach, California, event on June 9, 1962, when the Bay Area and Los Angeles Roadster Clubs got together for their second annual gathering. This picture was taken south of San Luis Obispo. I remember racing ahead on the freeway, stopping, and climbing a hill to take this picture as planned. Tex Smith from *Hot Rod* had the same idea, and we were side-by-side when this picture was taken! The lead "T" Touring was Norm Grabowski's. It later became "My Mother The Car" on a TV series of the same name. Following is Warren Freedlun in his '29 Ford, and behind him is Lee Barrett of the B.A.R.

Roadster Club members congregate in fellowship at our motel in Pismo Beach on June 9, 1962. The afternoon was hot, and the refreshments were cooling. When I took this picture I never realized that someday it would be a historic classic! Not happy with just a glass, Norm Grabowski sips his brew from a pitcher. I bet he was whistling at the same time; he use to do that and no one knew where the whistle came from! Who could whistle and drink at the same time? One person: Norm Grabowski! Norm was and still is quite the entertainer. In the chair facing Norm is Tom McMullen, L.A. member and future Publisher of *Street Rodder* and *Custom Rodder*. Sadly, Tom died in a plane crash in 1995.

"Kugie's Kar" comes from Hayward, California, and was owned by Don Kugler. When I first met Don he was already a Bay Area Roadster Club member. His '26 "T" roadster pickup is powered by a 356-ci 1953 Oldsmobile engine with a Hubbard cam, McGurk lifters and rockers, Toledo pistons, P.C. rings, and four Stromberg carbs set on an Edelbrock intake manifold. Don did all the work on his roadster, including the chromed outside-type headers. Don painted the roadster metallic blue, and I pinstriped it in white. The interior, top, and tarp on the pickup bed are Naugahyde. On June 16, 1962, I took pictures of the truck for Hot Rod (October '63 issue), and after the shooting, we stopped in this drive-in to have a bite to eat.

# Chapter 2
# 1963-1964

There was a British Invasion in the United States, but it was mostly limited to rock 'n' roll music. The Beatles and other top British bands made their mark in the States around 1963 and 1964, but customizers and hot rodders continued to enjoy their wheels American style. That not only meant flashier and flashier, but more and more futuristic as well.

LeRoi "Tex" Smith, took top honors at the 1963 Oakland Roadster Show with his "XR-6," a '27 Ford roadster that had touches of tomorrow despite its roots in America's automotive past. There was a throwback of sorts the next year at Oakland, though, as Don Tognotti was the big winner in 1964 with his '14 Ford roadster, the oldest model ever to win the America's Most Beautiful Roadster Award.

A muscular Chrysler 300J convertible paced the 1963 Indy 500, which was won by Parnelli Jones. Maybe you could say the British Invasion extended to Indianapolis, because Jim Clark drove a Lotus to second place in the 500, setting the tone for a new wave of British-built race cars that would dominate Indy. A hot new Ford Mustang convertible paced the 1964 race, which was won by A.J. Foyt.

In current events, the November 1963 assassination of President John F. Kennedy dominated the news and changed the nation forever. Actor Sidney Poitier made history by winning the Academy Award as Best Actor for the 1963 film "Lilies of the Field," and in 1964 a fairy tale nanny was honored as Julie Andrews was named Best Actress for her role in "Mary Poppins."

Joe Bailon Customs built this 1951 Ford Victoria for Joe Tocchini of Hayward, California. Radical customizing was done. The front end has a special cavity and pan housing a '57 Buick grille. The front fenders were flared and radiused, the headlight openings were frenched, and '57 Imperial quad lights were used. Up front are custom-made nerf bar/bumpers. A scoop was put in the hood and round rod was formed to make a depression leading down to the end of the hood. A custom built rocker panel has an opening for outside, chromed, lake-type plugs running to the rear of car. Wheels are chromed and reversed, and hubcaps are from a '50 Ford with bullet centers and six chromed blades. Bailon entered this custom as "El Tangerino" at Oakland in 1963.

This rear view of El Tangerino shows the rear fenderwells were radiused, and round rod was used to outline the contour back and around the rear fender, creating a hood over the taillights. Two '56 Oldsmobile taillights were used on each side. Notice that the trunk is reshaped to conform to the hooded bodywork over the taillights, and a light housing is molded to the trunk above the license plate. 1955 Pontiac split bumpers are used, and an area between the bumpers is filled with a molded panel. The interior has pleated-and-rolled Naugahyde with white buttons on a maroon frieze material. Bailon called it El Tangerino because he painted it pearl white with a candy tangerine top and lower contoured body panels.

Bill Cushenbery's futuristic show roadster "Silhouette" premiered in January 1963, at the San Mateo Autorama. I witnessed some of the construction in his Monterey shop, and I'm sorry I didn't take any pictures. Cushenbery and illustrator Don Varner created the Silhouette concept. Handmade of 20-gauge sheet metal, with an Acry Plastics blown bubble top, it has candy paint that is contoured in red, gold, and black lacquer. The chassis is that of a '56 Buick, shortened to a 98-inch wheelbase. The wheels are reversed Cadillac wheels with knock-off caps. The 1956 Buick engine has modified Hilborn fuel injection, and the transmission is a beefed-up Dynaflow. The special exhaust system was created by Tom Brown Mufflers of Seaside. The sculptured rear end has wrap-around taillights, the top opens with remote controls, and the upholstery is white Naugahyde by the master, Bill Manger.

"The Moonshiner," is what Mickey Himsl, from Concord, California, called his '26 Ford "T" half-a-touring-car-bodied roadster. Here it is at the January 1963 San Mateo Autorama, painted in Metalflake chartreuse and violet acrylic lacquer by Himsl. White Naugahyde upholstery was stitched by his brother, Art Himsl, the famous painter. The body is channeled 7 inches over a '30 Ford chassis. The suicide-style front end has a 3-inch dropped axle, 5.50 Dunlop tires, and mag wheels. There are M&H slick tires with American Mag wheels on the rear, and brakes are used on rear wheels only, heavy-duty Lincolns. A 5-gallon gas tank, made of a chromed can, sits on a rear cross-member. The '48 engine has a 3 3/8-inch bore and 4 1/4-inch stroke.

Richard Zocchi of Pittsburg, California, owns this 1962 Pontiac Grand Prix two-door hardtop on display at the San Mateo Autorama in January 1963. At the 1962 Oakland Roadster Show, Rich won the "Car D'Elegance" award. Customizer Gene Winfield performed all the custom work, including extending the outer headlights forward by 3 inches, and frenching and tunneling all four headlights with custom, handmade inner rims. The custom grilles were made up of perforated metal with a new type of bullet made exclusively for this car. All exterior chrome was removed from the Pontiac, and the car was lowered all around. In keeping with the current custom styling at that time, reversed chromed wheels were used. The Pontiac had only 52 miles on it when it was customized.

Here is a rear view of Rich Zocchi's '62 Pontiac Grand Prix. The trunk is free of emblems and Gene Winfield customized the fenders by extending the tips and reshaping and canting them inward. All other emblems and door handles were taken off, and the doors are operated electrically. Innovative for the time are the custom taillights, as the taillight lenses are from a '62 Chrysler Imperial, capped with small chromed bullets. The housings were completely custom made on a lathe, then chrome-plated. As always, the Winfield paint job was exceptional, pearl white with candy orange blends. The upholstery is pearl white Naugahyde with rolls and pleats. This is a fine example of a tastefully restyled 1960s custom.

The Oakland Roadster Show's "America's Most Beautiful Roadster" in 1962 was George Barris's '27 "T" roadster, which George named the "Twister T." Here it is as it appeared at the San Mateo Show of January 1963. Even as a show rod, it was driven, and it did pretty well when Rod & Custom did a road test for its August '63 issue. Running a stock '56 Dodge 270-ci V-8 with four 97 carburetors, the roadster clocked 80 miles per hour in 17 seconds. At 60 miles per hour it took 202 feet of braking to stop. The "T" body sits on a '32 Ford frame, and is painted peacock Metalflake lacquer. Upholstery is by Lee Wells of North Hollywood, in pearl white Naugahyde with matching peacock metal flake seat bottoms. The wire wheels are 15-inch Buicks.

After seeing the Oakland Roadster Show, Rudy Heredia said to himself, "Some day I have to build a rod," and that he did, a 1916 "T" bucket that he paid only $25 for! I met Rudy in the latter part of 1961, when his roadster was blue. I photographed it and it appeared (as seen here) in the August '62 issue of Rod & Custom. When it appeared in the San Jose Show in January, 1963, it was red. Rudy's "T" sits on a modified '31 chassis with a stock '32 Ford front axle and springs from a Model A. The engine is a '55 Buick that runs six carbs and has custom exhaust headers made by Rudy. The white tuck-and-roll upholstery is by Banning, and I did the pinstriping.

The National Hot Rod Association's (NHRA) Winternationals Car Show was held in Los Angeles in February 1963, and there I took this picture of Mox Miller's '58 Chevy Impala, which won first place in the Conservative Custom Coupe/Sedan class. The Chevy was bought new, it was stock-bodied and had a fabulous interior, with lots of chrome and a Dick Jackson paint job with Dennis Rickleffs pinstriping that was done in 1962. The engine has a Cragar blower with dual carbs, and the wheels are polished Halibrand Indy Mags.

Here's another 1963 Winternationals Car Show picture, but this time it's of people having fun! It's the Ford Caravan group showing how to play and maneuver the slot car races. As you can see by the smiles on all the faces, excitement was in the air! Shown here in the blue jackets are (left-right): Bud "The Kat from AMT" Anderson, from AMT Corporation, Troy, Michigan; Mike Alexander of Alexander Brothers Customs, Detroit, Michigan; and Bill Cushenbery of Cushenbery Customs. Even though it was all in fun, I wonder who won the races? Sorry to say, Bud Anderson passed away in 1993.

More than 70,000 people took in nearly 300 exhibits at the NHRA Winternationals Car Show in February 1963 in Los Angeles. The crowds broke the attendance record for the third annual show, and one exhibitor was Mel Taormino with his outstanding '29 Ford roadster pickup. The flawless bodywork was done by Wilhelm Customs of San Jose, and it was painted American LaFrance fire engine red lacquer. The engine is from a 1959 Chevy Corvette, with fuel injection, an Engle cam, and Hedman headers. Notice the dual master cylinders on the firewall, which operate the brake and clutch. The running boards are chromed, and the wire wheels are Chryslers with Royal Master tires. The transmission is from '39 Ford with Lincoln Zephyr gears, and the rear end is from '48 Mercury with a 4.11 ratio.

For many years I have had the pleasure of photographing the Oakland Roadster Show, the cars, the displays, and the last-night trophy presentations. Some years ago I received this picture taken by San Francisco photographer Pete Biro, who captured me (lower right) as I was also photographing an interview at the 1963 Roadster Show. I believe it was one of the very few times that these famous customizers were together in one place. They include (left-right): George Barris, Ed Roth, Darryl Starbird, Bill Neumann (editor of *Rod & Custom*), Gene Winfield, Bill Cushenbery, and Joe Wilhelm. The interview appeared in the July '63 issue of *Rod & Custom* along with photos Pete and I took that Saturday afternoon. *Author collection, courtesy Pete Biro*

L.A. Roadster Club member Walt Kaline of Whittier, California, owned this 1924 'glass-body "T" roadster. He was once asked why he built this, and his answer was, "I dig 'T' roadsters the most." Construction time was less than a year, and Walt chose a '56 Pontiac 317-ci engine with ported and polished heads and an Isky CC-606 cam. Walt built and chrome-plated the headers and radius rods, which was easy since Lustre Chrome Plating in Gardena, California, is his business. The transmission is a '56 Pontiac Hydro with a homemade shifter connecting to a '51 Mercury rear end with 3.11 gears. The steering is from a '42 Ford pickup, and the front axle, springs, and brake backing plates are all chromed. Black Naugahyde upholstery gives contrast to the pearl green lacquer paint.

At the Oakland Roadster Show of February 1963, I had the honor of photographing an exclusive interview with six of the world's best custom car builders, and it was a pleasurable two-hour chore! One of the custom car builders interviewed was Joe Wilhelm, from San Jose, California. In this picture are (left-right): Joe's wife Marion, Joe Wilhelm, and myself. Every year, Al Slonaker, producer of the show, hosted a luncheon for the show participants, the press, and the enthusiast magazines who covered the show. I represented *Rod & Custom* along with Editor Bill Neumann. This picture was taken at that luncheon reception. *Author collection, courtesy Eric Rickman*

I had known Bill Cushenbery for three years when I took this picture on February 24, 1963, the final night at the Oakland Roadster Show. It was indeed a pleasure seeing Bill win the Master Builder Award, Tournament Of Fame, with his futuristic "Silhouette" show roadster. Bill was the first to win this tournament, which offered a free trip to the Paris Auto Show with Al and Mary Slonaker. The competition was only open to bona fide custom builders. Prior to the Oakland Show, the Silhouette was painted candy red, gold, and black when it appeared in the January 1963 San Mateo Autorama. This picture shows it when it was a pearl lavender color.

During the November 1963, Roadster Roundup involving the Bay Area Roadsters and the L.A. Roadster Club at Pismo Beach, George Solimine of South San Francisco checked something out in his mirror. On his '29 Ford roadster pickup, George straightened the body, painted it Dodge royal blue, installed '48 Ford brakes and rear end, and ran a 286-ci Ford flathead with three Stromberg 97 carbs. The pickup bed was shortened and widened to match the body width, and the black-and-white pinstriping was done by Tommy the Greek. In the background is fellow B.A.R. member Rudy Perez, while Barbara Mendonca stands at left.

In the early 1960s, Darryl Starbird of Star Custom Show Cars submitted design sketches to Monogram Models, Inc., including one of a futuristic custom named "Futurista." The design was approved, and construction work began. Futurista has a full Lucite bubble top in two sections, an interior of red velvet with inset panels of stainless steel, and pearl white paint. It is a three-wheeler with center control steering, and push-button-operated brakes, throttle, and clutch. Mounted in the rear is an air-cooled Volkswagen Spyder engine, and the exhaust goes through the rear tube grille opening below the main horizontal design line. On the right in the picture is Darryl Starbird, talking to Jack Besser, president of Monogram at the Oakland Show in 1963.

Gene Winfield called his custom '50 Mercury "Solar Scene," as it was presented at the Oakland Show of 1963. The headlights are frenched, tunneled, and offset 3 inches using Lucas quad lights. The grille shell has been molded with custom-chromed tubular grilles, and front pans house a flat-type bumper. The wheelwells are extensively reworked, in a teardrop shape with a new style of flair incorporated; polished sheet metal was formed to accomplish this. The engine is a stock '56 Buick Century dolled up with a lot of chrome, including the radiator and the steering column. Gene chopped the Merc 3 1/2 inches in front, 4 1/2 inches in the rear. A one-piece '54 Mercury windshield was used.

America's Most Beautiful Roadster of 1963 was owned by LeRoi "Tex" Smith, associate editor of *Hot Rod*. The design concept for his XR-6 custom creation was done by Steve Swaja, and work was performed by Barris Kustoms, Gene Winfield, Gordon Van's Body Shop, and Tex himself. A detailed analysis appeared in the August 1963 issue of *Hot Rod*, and it featured a "phantom" view in color, showing the frame and all the components and how things were put together. The body started out as a '27 "T," it's mounted on a tube frame, and it has a Volkswagen front end and a Dodge Dart aluminum slant-six engine with a Torqueflite tranny and Dodge rear end. Beige Naugahyde upholstery was done by Tony Nancy, and the paint was candy tangerine Metalflake.

I did not realize until I was working on this book that this fabulous 1958 Ford Thunderbird had belonged to my friend Hershel "Junior" Conway of the House Of Color. It is seen here at the L.A. Winternationals Car Show in February 1964. Junior formed the grille out of electrical conduit, then had it chromed. The hood has custom touches such as rounded corners, and the air scoop is extended. Headlights are stock '58 T-Bird lights with the headlight doors reworked. All the chrome trim was stripped from the sides, the door corners have been rounded, and deep-dish 7-inch Astro wheels were new on the market. The rear fins were shortened and rounded, and the taillights were from a Dodge Dart. Black tuck-and-roll upholstery is by Eddie Martinez, and the candy red paint with Metalflake top is by Junior himself.

Here's a three-quarter rear view of the '40 Ford Tudor sedan of Steve Hill of Lynwood, California, as it looked while shown at the 1964 L.A. Winternationals show. The sedan is basically stock-bodied, except for the Barris-radiused and -flared edges on the front fenderwells. Barris shot photos and produced a "how-to" magazine article while working on Steve's fenders. The beautiful candy red paint job was done by Hershel "Junior" Conway. Chromed reverse wheels with baldy hubcaps present a nice contrast. Beneath the hood sits a 303.73-ci '53 Olds "98" V-8, and the transmission is a '40 Ford with 25-tooth Zephyr gears with a 4.11 rear-end ratio. It ran pretty well, too, doing 80 miles per hour in fifteen seconds.

Bob Larivee, Sr., president of the Show Car Division of Promotions, Inc., commissioned Bill Cushenbery to build the *Car Craft* Dream Rod, which took 15 months to complete. The all-metal body was fabricated with sheet metal and panels from a Pontiac and Corvair. Offset styling was the new trend, as seen here, and a modified Jowett-Jupiter frame was used, stepped 18 inches in the rear, while a '51 VW torsion front end is used. A suspended pod holds the dual lights, and the opening has a meshed, filled grille. The engine is a 1963-1/2 289-ci Ford, backed by a four-speed transmission with a Hurst floor shifter. Wire wheels from a '63 T-Bird were adapted to VW and Jowet T-Jupiter hubs. These photos were taken August 30, 1963.

Another view of the *Car Craft* Dream Rod shows oval tube nerf bars that protect the right side at both front and rear, and like the headlights, a single taillight lights up the left side. Chromed outside exhaust pipes run under the panel by the door. Manger did all the fine upholstery in pearl white and beige Naugahyde, and restyled Triumph bucket seats are used. The dash cluster is from '57 Mercury, and it rests between the padded cowl and custom console. A rectangular steering wheel was designed from round and oval tubing, and it's connected to a modified Kharmann Ghia steering column. The candy paint is pearlescent sand and gold lacquer.

Pinky Richards of Whittier, California, owned this 1957 Corvette, on which customizer Bill Hines of Lynwood did the bodywork, such as filling in the body scoops and air vents. Taillights are from a '60 Mercury, recessed in the top of the fenders, and custom chromed nerf bars replace the original bumperettes. The hubcaps are from a Buick Riviera, the body has been completely de-chromed, the interior is done in black leather and fur by Eddie Martinez of Lynwood, and under the dash is an ARC record player. Tagged as "Watson's Wildest," Larry Watson of Paramount, California, did the paint job in candy orange Metalflake with dark green flames and yellow pinstriping. Can you imagine a "For Sale" price of $1,995.00? This photo was taken February 1964, at the Winternationals Car Show.

Although these flames look like Larry Watson's style on this 1955 Chevy Nomad station wagon, Larry did not recall doing the flames and didn't know who the car belonged to, but the wagon was too nice to eliminate from this book, so I'm presenting it without the owner's name. Painted a dark purple, with lavender and pearl-shaded flames, it's very striking! The roof is Metalflake, which was popular during that time. Extra '53 Chevy teeth adorn the grille cavity, and the Nomad is lowered and sports chromed wire wheels. The photo was shot at the Winternationals Car Show in 1964.

Customizer Bill Cushenbery was with the Ford Caravan team, and had the pleasure of customizing a 1963 Ford convertible, which was called "The Astro." The front and rear has similar styling, and frenched, deep circular openings housed vertical Lucas headlights. A chromed bar passes through the oval headlight housings between the headlights and on to the other side, and a Ford emblem is in the middle of the grille opening. Stock taillights are frenched and tunneled into the fenders, and a single bar is suspended in the rear grille cavity. The rear fenderwells were opened up to match the front, and custom chrome wheels are used. Bill painted the Astro ice blue pearl lacquer, and Bill Manger did the upholstery in pearl white Naugahyde.

You might say this is a very rare shot, so I'm so glad I can share this picture with you readers! It was taken on move-in day at the Los Angeles Winternationals, February 1964, and Joe Wilhelm with his wife Marion were getting the "Wild Dream" roadster ready for the upcoming weekend. Show promoters supplied a turntable for the car. It took Joe three years to build this custom roadster, and it was done originally for John Fernandez, but Joe ended up owning the roadster. Under the hood is a 283-ci '60 Chevy engine, and the car has a '61 Chevy four-speed transmission and a '56 Mercury rear end with 3.31 gears. Banning of Gilroy did the black Naugahyde upholstery, and the paint was Joe's favorite color, violet Metalflake lacquer.

Prevalent during those years were girls who had some nice customs, and one such gal was Beverly Gregg of Sacramento, California, who showed her 1957 Ford Thunderbird at the Oakland Roadster Show in February 1964. The custom headlights were taken from a '56 Oldsmobile, and the front grille opening was custom made, with expanded metal in the background. Fixed to the expanded metal are eight medium-sized chrome bullets, with 37 little chrome bullets surrounding the grille cavity. Directional lights are to each side. The rear fenderwells were radiused to match the front fenderwells, chromed wheels with knock-off style hubs are used, and the taillights are from a '58 Edsel. The interior has white Naugahyde tuck-and-roll upholstery, and the paint is candy red Metalflake with gold highlights.

In late-1958, Larry Sanford of Glendale, California, took his 1940 Mercury four-door convertible to Valley Custom Shop in Burbank, where Neil Emory and Clayton Jensen sectioned 4 inches from the top portion of the doors, rolling the tops to meet the window openings. The rear doors and back cowl section were done the same way, and the windshield was chopped approximately 3 inches. Recently I talked with Neil and found out the trunk lid was also shortened 7 inches. At the rear, the top of the body was reworked to eliminate the high crown it had when stock. In 1960, Neil left Valley Customs and Clayton painted the Mercury metallic green before the shop closed. This was just about the last car to be done by Valley Customs, and this picture was taken at the Winternationals Show, February 1964.

George Barris's "Villa Riviera" started out as a '63 Buick, and it was styled and built by George in his Hollywood shop. The front end was extended over 6 inches and was V-shaped, while two grille cavities, canted bars, and strips match the trim on the hood. The headlights carry the same theme. The Landau-style top is cantilevered and covered in white alligator hide, and the front part of top is removable. Front and rear fenderwells are radiused, and extra-deep-dish Astro wheels accept 10 1/2-inch wide General three-band whitewall tires. The interior is white leather with walnut grain paneling. The paint color is candy cherry red, as it appeared here in the Oakland Roadster Show of 1964. Movie star James Darren used the Buick in the movie *For Those Who Think Young*.

Parked on the patio lawn during the Monterey Kar Kapades in March 1964, was Bob McNulty's '55 Corvette named "Sharkamino." Bob, killed years later in a boating accident, originally bought the 'Vette in Texas as a wreck for $ 1600. Reworking it and adding to the fiberglass body, he made a custom nose piece and grille, and the front fenders have recessed side panels of aluminum punched with reversed louvers. The rear flared fins have red Lucite taillights, and a special bed was built between the fins. Custom-chromed nerf bars are found front and rear, and the paint is candy lime lacquer. It has a '63 Corvette engine with a four-speed transmission and positraction rear end. To the left is the Oldsmobile-powered '40 Ford pickup of Pete Paulsen, owner of House Of Wheels in San Leandro, California.

Joe Botti of Redwood City first gained notoriety with his 1954 Ford pickup when it appeared on the August 1956, *Rod & Custom* cover. Featuring Tommy the Greek Iris blue-and-purple paint scallops, the car received awards at the Oakland, Monterey, San Jose, and Fresno car shows. Here it is at the Monterey Kar Kapades in March 1964, and I haven't seen it since then! It was restyled in 1956 with a modified grille opening, quad headlights, and expanded metal mesh with a Chrysler grille. It had chromed wheels and chromed running boards, and underneath and along the side boards are dual chromed exhausts. The interior has black Naugahyde upholstery, and a pleated boot over the bed. A custom rear pan holds four square taillights. This pickup has impeccable Tommy the Greek pinstriping, and the paint is gorgeous candy apple red scallops on black.

Besides roadsters, I also dug tourings! In May 1964, I shot a few pictures of the 1928 Ford Touring car I owned. Originally built in Los Angeles by John Holmes, I was able to acquire the Touring and do some changes to my liking. It was jet black lacquer, and I put in a 1958 283-ci Chevy backed by a three-speed transmission. The rear end had a Halibrand quick-change center section with Helicoil gears for quietness. The interior is pleated black Naugahyde, done by Pasadena Top Shop, and the dash has eight Stewart Warner instruments. The front end has a dropped axle, and reworked '40 Ford spindles with reversed spring eyes. The brakes are from a '40 Ford, and the reversed chromed wheels and hubcaps are from a '50 Mercury.

Being associated with the Bay Area Roadster Club for many years, we had the opportunity to do some good deeds! On a Sunday in May 1964, we went to Letterman General Hospital at the Presidio of San Francisco, a facility for servicemen. The American National Red Cross, Golden Gate Chapter, invited us to bring our cars so the soldiers could view them in the parking lot. We had about 15 to 20 roadsters, which were enjoyed by all. Two favorites were (left) Tut Brown's Chevy-powered '29 Ford roadster, and (right) Paul Hannon's Studebaker-powered, channeled '29 Ford roadster.

This three-quarter rear view of Terry Corp's '56 Ford shows the same styling with the pan and grille work as in the front. The taillights customized to fit the rear fenders are from a '62 Dodge. The accenting color inside the side trim is pearl white and is carried on into the trunk lid. Nineteen-sixty Ford hubcaps are mounted over chromed reverse wheels, and the tires are U.S. Royal Masters, which were very popular at that time. All the bodywork was done the old-fashioned way, in lead, and credit goes to Ken's Body Shop in Salinas. Metalflake gold with pearl lacquer was applied by Karcich Customs of Castroville. The upholstery and dash were done in pearl white Naugahyde, and the doors and trunk are electrically operated.

Living in Salinas, the same town as car owner Terry Corp lived in, I saw this '56 Ford Tudor sedan customized three times. It went from burgundy to pink to Metalflake lime gold. Proud owner Terry is standing next to his Ford, which has front rolled pans that are from a '53 Studebaker, and a grille fabricated from expanded metal using cabinet handle ornamentation. Quad headlights are frenched and canted outward utilizing '57 Ford rings with '61 Ford taillight frames. The antenna in the left front fender is the telescoping type, and '57 Pontiac side trim was altered to fit evenly into the taillights. The engine is a '63 Ford with an Isky 505 cam and an AFB carb. There's an 11-inch clutch, and the transmission is from a '57 Ford.

As I was reviewing my material for this book, I came across this June 6, 1964, picture taken in Fresno by L.A. Roadster Club President and good friend Dick Scritchfield. I was on a rod run with the Bay Area Roadsters. During this era I was taking pictures for pleasure and to expand my archives. The camera I used during this time was a twin-lens Mamiyaflex with a Heiland strobe light. Little did I realize that eventually I would have approximately 58,000 pictures in my archives. I wonder if my cigarette got in the way when I was taking pictures? *Author collection, courtesy of Dick Scritchfield*

# Chapter 3
# 1965-1966

Things were getting a little wild by the mid-1960s, as more and more customizers tried their hands at building the cars of tomorrow: futuristic vehicles with new shapes and lines, bubble tops, and electronics. Yet one good thing about the custom and hot rod scene is that it will never completely desert its roots, so we still saw plenty of great-looking, beautifully crafted "traditional" rods and customs.

One of these was Don Lokey's '27 Ford roadster, which in 1966 was named America's Most Beautiful Roadster at the Oakland Roadster Show. Don's creation certainly had some modern, sleek touches, but at the root of it all was a tried-and-true Henry Ford masterpiece.

The 1965 winner at the Oakland show was Carl Casper, whose "Ghost," a custom fiberglass roadster, opened the crowd's eyes to some new ideas.

The 1965 winner at the Indy 500 was also an eye-opener, as Jim Clark drove a mid-engined Lotus to an easy victory, signaling the end of the front-engined roadster era at Indianapolis. Another British driver, Graham Hill, won at Indy in 1966, the same year another Indiana treasure, the University of Notre Dame, won the national college football championship. And actress Elizabeth Taylor won the Oscar for Best Actress for "Who's Afraid of Virginia Woolf?"

On Sunday, April 24, 1966, the Bay Area Roadster Club had an outing at Mount Madonna Park, near Watsonville, California. It was a gathering for the members, their wives or girlfriends, and the kids, and fun was had by all! Of course, I had my trusty Leica camera along and took some pictures, and here are a couple Bay Area Roadsters of outstanding quality. To the left is Warren Freedlun's '29 Ford roadster, with a 283-ci Chevy using a Clay Smith cam and six 97 carbs. Tan Naugahyde upholstery accents the American LaFrance Fire Engine red paint. On the right is John Hansen's '29 Ford roadster, which is 327-ci Chevy powered and has its body on a '32 frame. Its upholstery is black Naugahyde, and its paint is vintage burgundy. It also looks like John was experimenting with some chrome wire wheels.

With the help of customizer Darryl Starbird, Bob Greenwade of Blackwell, Oklahoma, turned his 1964 Corvette into the "Cosma Ray," and it was named Best Custom at the 1964 National Custom Auto Fair in Indianapolis, Indiana. The nose of the Cosma Ray is peaked, and has a custom grille, quad headlights behind a Lucite cover, and a custom scoop on the hood. The wheelwells were opened up, flared, and repositioned, and chromed Astro wheels are fitted with Firestone tires. Custom-built chromed side pipes go the length of the rocker panels. The car has a 327-ci Corvette engine with an Isky 505 cam and Mickey Thompson pistons, lifters, and rocker arms. This photo was taken at the San Jose Autorama on January 16, 1965.

Over the years as I photographed rods and customs, I've been noted for having attractive models pose with the cars, and it was no exception with my own roadster. This picture was taken on January 10, 1965, as I did a photo shoot of my '29 Ford roadster for *Hot Rod*, which published the photos in its July issue. Lovely model Patria Pere appeared in the feature, not sitting on the back of the seat, but on the running board. The camera was on a tripod to take this picture, as I am showing Patria how I wanted her to pose. Incidentally, my roadster was Chevy powered, with multiple carbs, and ran a Duntov cam. I applied the rustic maroon paint and gold-and-white pinstriping myself.

The 1965 San Jose Autorama featured Don and Millie Lokey's "T+II" '27 T-roadster pickup. Don is from Fresno, home of California Chrome, where all the plating was done. Barris Kustoms did all the restyling work, which consists of a one-piece grille shell with Cibie headlights canted with the shell and a floating '15 Model T radiator inside the grille shell. The handmade air cleaners are styled as per the grille opening, and the engine is from a '57 Corvette. It has a Lincoln transmission, a Ford rear end that is completely chromed, and a tube-type chassis. The rear panel and bed are sculptured into one piece with small finned fenders and a recessed tailgate. The interior is pearl white Naugahyde, and the paint is candy cherry over pearl. In 1966, Don's "T" won America's Most Beautiful Roadster honors.

If memory serves me right, our club had 12 roadsters entered in the Winternationals Car Show in Los Angeles on January 1965, at the Pan Pacific Auditorium. As shown, we had a big banner that stretched between the columns where our roadsters were parked. Seen here are (left-right): Ed Huff's purple '23 T; Dick Mendonca's black '29 Ford; my maroon '29 Ford; Lee Barrett's brown '29 Ford; Rudy Heredia's red '23 T; Dave Marasco's black '29 Ford; and Don Kugler's blue '27 T.

San Jose Roadster Club member Vince Burgos built his '29 Ford roadster the traditional way, full-fendered and with a hood and a top. He did the bodywork and painted it in anniversary gold lacquer, while under the hood is a 283-ci Chevy with a single AFB carb. It has a 3-inch dropped front axle, hydraulic brakes, a stick-shift transmission with Lincoln gears, and a '48 Ford rear end. Ford spinners give the Plymouth wire wheels a knock-off look. Bill Clenendon did the black, pleated-and-rolled Naugahyde interior and the white nylon top. The car was photographed in September 1965.

Lee Jue wanted to customize his '65 Ford Thunderbird, but he didn't know how, so he took it to Dean Jeffries to do the job. Dean came up with some sketches, and "The Seaburst," as it was called, was under way. Dean stretched the nose a full 10 inches, adding sheet metal to the hood and fenders, and crafting a new opening for a grille and headlights. Four chromed flat-stock bars became the grille, and in back were a pair of Falcon headlights. The simulated hood scoop was opened and extended, and the rear fenderwell openings were slightly enlarged. In the rear, the grille opening was formed as at the front end, and handmade Lucite taillights are behind the grille work. The paint is pearl mint green with granules of cut glass added.

Fred Marasco of Monterey owned this '23 T roadster, which took more than two years to build, and I watched the project from the beginning until it was finished, snapping this photo in January 1965. Fred made his frame from boxed tubing, with a 7-inch kick-up just ahead of the rear end. Stainless steel was snug-fitted to the frame and engine-turned. A '37 Ford tube axle graces the front, with homemade brackets to hold the Airheart disc brakes, and the rear of the chassis has four Monroe Load-Leveler shocks. The wheels are E.T. mags. An Oldsmobile F-85 high performance V-8 was used, the transmission is a Borg Warner four-speed, and it has a '64 Ford pickup rear end. The body was laminated for strength, and painted forest green lacquer. Banning did the platinum pearl upholstery.

This 1956 Lincoln Continental belongs to the combo of Gary Lee and Lee Wells of North Hollywood, California. It was acquired from Gary Lee's godfather, Alex Dreyer, the famous Chicago news commentator. Gary and Lee wanted a radical custom, so they took it to Jack McKay, who channeled the body 5 inches. The front and rear bumpers were sectioned; the grille shell is from a Mercedes and has 1/4-inch aluminum bars and a Lincoln emblem. The engine is stock, and is Hilborn-injected. The headlights are frenched with Lucas lights, and the double bubble top is by Acry Plastics. Heavy custom wheels are from Walker Aluminum Foundry, and the swivel bucket seats are in pearl-hued leather. Junior Conway sprayed marigold Metalflake lacquer paint. This photo was shot at the Winternationals Car Show in January 1965, and it was named Best Experimental in the show.

When I took this picture in June 1965 of Fred Marasco sitting in his T, it was along 17 Mile Drive near Pebble Beach. When the weather was nice, we drove our roadsters as often as we could, and Fred and I, both members of the Bay Area Roadster Club, enjoyed our roadsters fully. I remember going to Los Angeles and taking many parts to Lustre Chrome Plating, where owner Walt Kaline did a fantastic job. Can you imagine going 600-and-some-odd miles to get chrome done? Well, Fred did, and it was worth the trip.

A longtime friend and another Bay Area Roadster Club member is David Marasco, who is standing besides his immaculate '29 Ford roadster pickup. As with his brother Fred's roadster, I saw this truck being built through the stages until the 4th of July weekend of 1962, when it was first started up. Dave's roadster is Chevy powered, has a '39 Ford tranny, and a Ford rear with 4.11 gears. The chromed front end has a dropped axle, hydraulic brakes, a louvered apron, and the pickup bed has been shortened 12 inches. On the jet black body, I did the red-and-white pinstriping. Today, my friend Greg Sharp owns this roadster—and the pinstriping is still there! In this photo, Dave and his roadster were participating in a B.A.R. function at the Winternationals Car Show in January 1965. Notice the official club jacket with the patch on the pocket.

Bill Burke (right) talks with a Reynolds Aluminum representative about the "Reynolds Aluminum Special" at the Los Angeles Winternationals in January 1965. Reynolds expressed an interest in the car when advised that the streamliner's skin was to consist of aluminum. Dick Dean of La Puente hand-formed the aluminum body. A 2x4-inch boxed frame of mild steel with a roll bar cage of chromoly tubing was built by Bill Burke himself. The front suspension is based on a tubular axle with Dragmaster torsion bars, and is controlled by friction shocks. The rear end is from a '48 Ford, with a Halibrand center section with 3.27 Getz gears. A destroked 300-ci Hemi was to be used for record attempts in the C Class at Bonneville, while other Chrysler Hemi engines would be used for record attempts in the B and D Class.

Raymond Goulart of Stockton, California, owned this customized '50 Oldsmobile. It was originally a convertible, but Ray added a hardtop and lowered the car all around. Ray did all the work himself, reshaping the front grille opening and installing a multitude of chromed round rod. In this picture the grille looks like it has been changed to a four-bar arrangement. Quad headlights are still the same with a modified '55 Oldsmobile bumper. Ray installed a 1959 Buick 410-ci engine with an Offenhauser manifold with dual carbs, and Offenhauser valve covers. Ray's original wheels were chrome-plated with bullet centers. This picture was taken when George Hill of Arizona owned it.

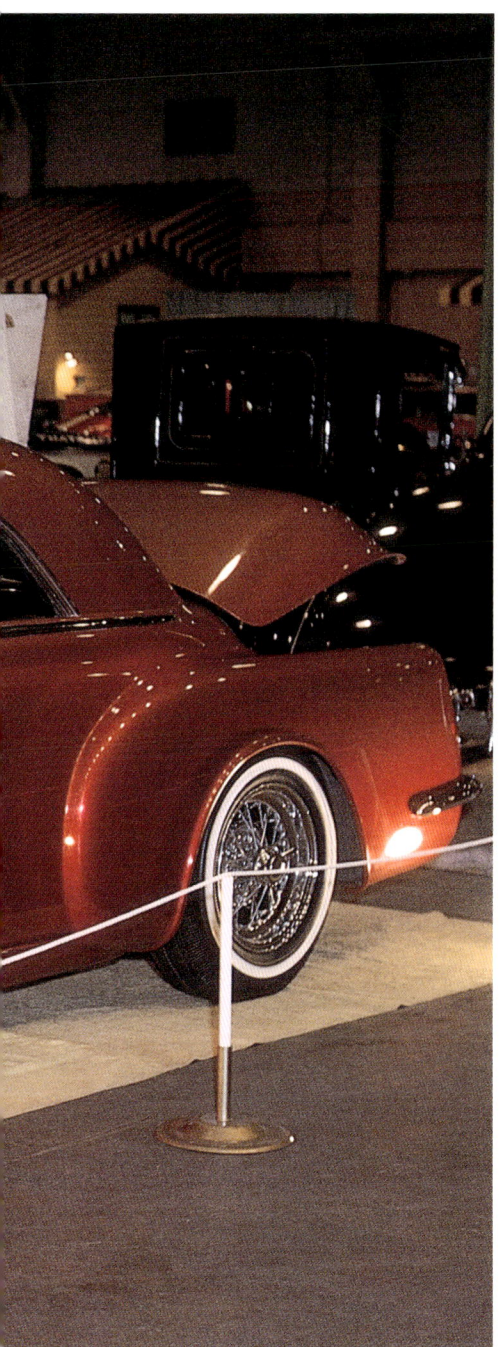

Allen King of Bell, California, built and owned this channeled '28 Ford roadster pickup with a bobbed rear bed. Being a painter by trade, Allen sprayed his roadster "Astroid Copper Metalflake" lacquer. His display sign says it's "The Copper Cart!" Being prolific as he was, he also did all the extra-fine stitch work on his pearl beige Naugahyde interior and bed cover. Other interior changes include a fitted '32 Ford dash with Stewart Warner gauges. The engine stuck between the frame is a 354-ci '54 Chrysler with a Clay Smith cam, and push rods and lifters are used with Chrysler Marine rockers and Mickey Thompson rods and pistons. The front axle, springs, backing plates, headers, and rear end were chromed by Model Plating Company.

It's Showtime! That's what Doug Vido of Van Nuys, California, thought when he entered his 1960 Pontiac Catalina hardtop in the Winternationals Car Show of 1965. Larry Watson painted the car candy butterscotch over pearl, and as was the trend at the time, he fogged the highlights in candy tangerine. The "Iron Indian," as it was called, was lowered all the way, in true custom car fashion. Skinny whitewall tires enhance the extremely wide Astro wheels with bullet centers. Lucas headlights sit inside chromed headlight frames, and stock rear taillights were frenched, while the side chrome was removed and the gas filler cap was filled in. Doug was President of the Chancellors Car Club.

The 1964 T-Bird was new when it was purchased by the uncle of Don Lorero of Walnut Creek, California. What a nice present! His uncle told him, "If you want a custom, let's take it to Joe Bailon." Joe extended the hood scoop 2 1/2 inches with a curved open front edge of round rod. The stock grille was replaced with 30 custom-fitted, chromed, vertical round rod grille bars, and pans were made to fit from the grille edges to the underside of the front fenders. Stock rear taillights were frenched, and fenderwells were opened and flared. Chrome wheels are from Astro, with gold center knock-offs. The interior is pearl white Naugahyde, and the paint is by Bailon in candy royal blue Metalflake. This picture taken at the 1965 Oakland Roadster Show.

This is one of my original, unpublished pictures of Ray Goulart's '50 Oldsmobile, taken on May 8, 1964. This three-quarter rear view shows the beautiful and extensive work done to the taillights, which had extended rear fenders with frenched '58 Oldsmobile lenses. The trunk was decked off and small handles were affixed to each side, which kept hands off the paint when closing deck lid. A rear pan was rolled underneath with recess for the license plate, and the rear bumper is from a '56 Buick. The front fenders have a flared scoop, which matched the flared fenderwells, and the rears were also radiused with a flared edge. The paint is candy copper, and the interior is of black Naugahyde by Scenic Auto of Modesto.

The sign in front says "Merc On The Wild Side," which described Rod Powell's '51 Mercury coupe, on display here at the 1965 Oakland Roadster Show. Swapping a Buick for the Mercury, Rod had quite a lot of work to do before it was finished as seen here. With a chopped top, added concave fenderwells, and a sculptured rear end, it was finished out a little more with the help of Bill Cushenbery. Custom, frenched, handmade taillights were put into an extended fender, and a rolled pan and grillework matched the front end. A sculptured rear deck accommodates the license plate. The headlights are frenched with quad lights and Lucite covers. Howard Curry did the black Naugahyde upholstery, and the Chrysler front seats actually swivel. The paint is candy tangerine lacquer, with fogging that's a shade darker.

Here's Rod Powell's Mercury in an unpublished photo of 25-year-old Rod. This photo was taken on February 11, 1965, two weeks before Rod entered his car in the Oakland Roadster Show. This was the day I photographed the car for a feature that appeared in the June 1965, issue of *Rod & Custom*. Even though I knew who he was, I met Rod in Don Varner's garage in Salinas in 1958, when Don was pinstriping Rod's '39 Chevy coupe. We got along well, and have been close friends ever since. Rod always loved to spray paint, years later he had his own shop, and he is now known all over the world.

This picture is a special one! Not just because of the roadster, but because this is one of only two or three pictures I have of Al Slonaker, the Oakland Roadster Show originator and director. This February 27, 1965, picture shows Al standing in the aisle at the show, wearing the dark jacket, undoubtedly talking with the two fellows about the show. Incidentally, the roadster belongs to Charles Miller of Norwalk, California. Nicknamed "Pointless," it's a '23 Ford T roadster pickup with a modified '60 Buick engine, three-speed transmission, and quick-change rear end. It has lots of chrome and candy pearl blue paint.

For me, being a member of the Bay Area Roadster Club was a joy and an honor. I participated in many roadster events and in car shows with the club during the 16 years I was a member. The majority of the time when we went on roadster runs we met at a specified member's home before we left. This picture was taken in May of 1965, and some of the members cars parked at the curb include (left-right): Lee Barrett's '29 Ford; Ed Huff's '23 Ford; my '29 Ford; Bill Marshall's '32 Ford; and Darrell Pinkerton's '29 Ford. Our destination? Unknown!

This roadster is such a classic! Duane Kofoed of Burbank owned the roadster and that's him with the "happy smile and the wave." The famous Dick Flint roadster had been updated with a 1961 Corvette 352-ci engine, dual quads, Vertex magneto, and Schiefer flywheel and clutch, all backed with a Corvette transmission. This is not a posed picture. Duane was getting into his roadster when I yelled at him. He waved, smiled, and I couldn't have asked for a better moment. The picture was taken at a Bay Area and Los Angeles Roadster Roundup in Fresno on June 12, 1965.

The "Golden State T," a 1919 T roadster, was owned by Don Specht (left), a member of the Bay Area Roadster Club who built it over a six-year period with his father. They built a frame out of 1 1/2x2-inch square tubing, putting Model A front suspension up front. The brakes are from a '49 Mercury, and the rear end is an all-chromed stock Chevrolet setup. It is powered by a 283-ci Chevy engine using fuel-injection pistons, and carburetion is two four barrels. Don made his own nerf bars and radiator, then had the radiator gold-plated. Firestone tires are mounted on Cragar wheels. The paint is vintage burgundy and black lacquer, and Al's Trim Shop of Fresno did the metal flake silver leather interior. This photo was taken in Fresno on June 12, 1965.

The '29 Ford roadster pickup of Jim Miraglia from San Leandro, California. Under the hood is a '55 Oldsmobile 400-ci with a Chet Herbert roller cam, dual Rochester quads, and a Mallory ignition. The transmission is a '39 Ford floor shifter with 25-tooth Lincoln gears. The rear end is from a '48 Merc with a 3.23 ratio, and the wheels are 15-inch American mags. The body and paint work was done by Al Rodia of San Leandro, and the Naugahyde upholstery is by Glenn Strutz of San Leandro. A lot of credit goes to San Leandro and to Jo Dee Kinnard, Miss San Leandro 1965.

One of my longtime buddies, Bob Kraus, by his channeled '32 Ford five-window coupe in September, 1965. The coupe was not completed with a full paint job, and Bob was standing in front of some primered bodywork. The engine is a 322-ci '55 Buick with an Offenhauser intake manifold and three 94s on top. The transmission is a Chevy four-speed, and the rear end was from a '56 Chevy.

When I went to Los Angeles, I usually stayed with Dick Scritchfield of Glendale. We had become good friends and his hospitality was wonderful. On a trip in August 1965, I pinstriped Dick's '32 Ford roadster for the first time. I pinstriped it a second time when he repainted it black some years later. Dick's roadster was the first that was painted a fine (No. 2) Metalflake red, and it was sprayed by Bill Kaegle of Eagle Rock under the supervision of Fred Bell of the Dobeckmun Co., originators of Metalflake. At the time I thought it was fun, and now I feel very honored to have pinstriped Dick's famous '32 with white striping.

Bill Marshall came from the custom and hot rod hub of Vacaville, California, and he turned this once-crashed roadster into a show winner. Bill, a B.A.R member, posed for me by wiping down the stock Buick V-8 with a four-barrel carb. The front end of this great street cruiser was chromed, it had a 2 1/2-inch dropped front axle, hydraulic brakes, a '39 Ford transmission, and a '48 Ford rear end.

This view of Barris's "Mystique" shows the rear end and how it follows the same theme as the front. The trunk is extended 12 inches, the fenders are stretched 8 inches, again forming a "W" design. The taillights are set inside the grille, and sculptured lines also run into the rear fenders with accenting tangerine blends. The rear has been lowered 5 inches, while the top has been chopped 2 1/2 inches in the front, with a 1 1/2-inch slanted windshield to emphasize sleekness. The roof has an electric American Sunroof, and a pull handle pops up when one end of a flush door handle is pressed. The wheels are chromed Radars with walnut spokes and combined walnut and chrome knock-off hubs. The interior has saddle tan leather upholstery.

When Gary Calvert of Salinas, California, bought this 1956 Oldsmobile hardtop in 1960, it was still in its stock colors, yellow and white. Soon thereafter, customizing was done, as Rod Powell designed the identically styled headlights and taillights, which were built by Willie Wilde, who also did other bodywork. The teardrop antenna is hidden, and the door handles have been removed so the doors are operated electronically. The grille opening is stock, with expanded metal with horizontal and vertical bars making up the grille cavity along with stainless steel edging. Nineteen-sixty three Buick Riviera wheels are used. Rod Powell and Dutch Waymier painted the candy red pearl paint, and there's silver Metalflake in the headlight and taillight housings. The interior is black Naugahyde, done by Gary and Ken Corral. This picture was taken at the 1966 San Mateo Show.

Dewey O'Connell of Santa Rosa, California, displayed his 1928 Ford roadster pickup at the San Mateo Autorama in January 1966. It was painted a sierra gold lacquer and had black diamond tuft Naugahyde upholstery. Following the trend of the "Ala Kart," Dewey punched 40 louvers in the side aprons below the door, and it looks like he has 24 or more louvers on the inner portions of the front fenders. The front end is chromed, and has a tube-type axle, front springs, shocks, and wishbones that are split. The front nerf bars are custom made, and the Goodyear tires are mounted on polished aluminum wheels. The engine is from a '60 Pontiac with triple carbs, and it runs an Iskenderian cam, while the transmission is a Pontiac Hydro, backed up to '48 Ford rear end.

During another trip to Los Angeles in February 1966, I visited Dick Scritchfield, who is shown here in his newly finished 1932 Ford phaeton. Dick originally obtained the phaeton from Eddie Ford in Australia, who shipped it to Dick at the San Pedro dock, where it came off the freighter W.R. Lundgren. Everything was there—except the engine. George Munson did all the bodywork, Eddie Martinez did the black islon upholstery, and I had the pleasure of applying pinstriping in gold on the beltline and hood side panels. The engine was a 289-ci Ford from a Mustang and Cobra, backed up by an automatic transmission to an Oldsmobile rear end. Dick still has the phaeton today and lives in Hawaii.

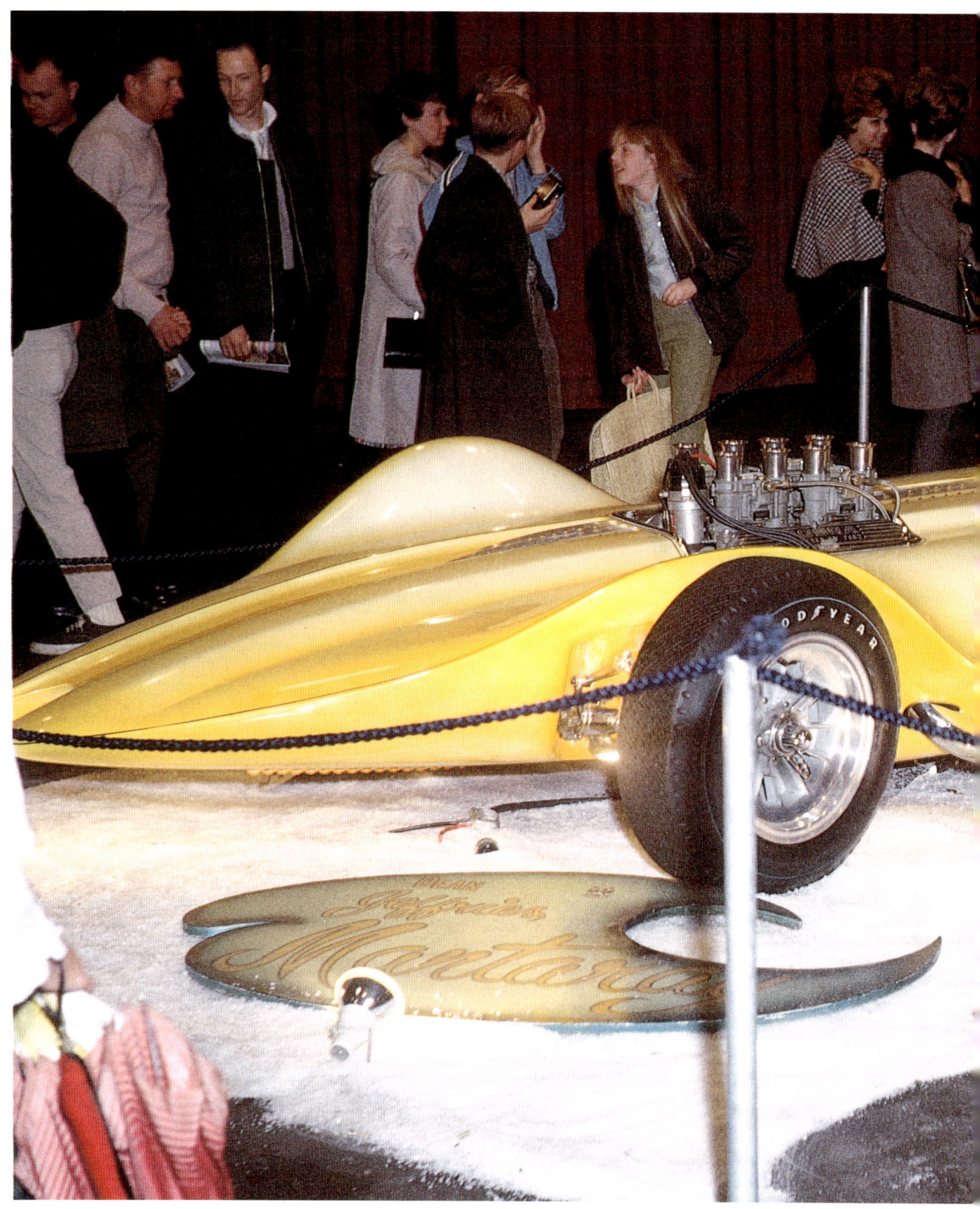

When Dean Jeffries won the Tournament of Fame Championship at the 1964 Oakland Roadster Show, I took a picture of him standing next to his winner, "The Mantaray." In this photo from two years later, the Mantaray has changed color to pearl yellow. This picture was taken February 5, 1966, at the Winternationals Car Show in Los Angeles. The engine is a Ford Fairlane 289 with Cobra racing modifications by Carroll Shelby. Weber carbs are used, and the ignition is a Mallory. The chassis is from a prewar Gran Prix Maseratti, and it has 15-inch finned Maseratti brakes. The body is aluminum, hand-formed by Dean along with Jim Burrell. The interior consists of separate pieces of leather that have been stretched, padded, and sewn together to form the entire unit. Goodyear tires are used on polished Halibrand wheels.

Steve Lykken of Buellton, California, has a most unique way of displaying his Cal-Automotive fiberglass '23 T Roadster. It is shown on an immaculate wood trailer in this photo from February 1966. This was the first roadster for Steve, and it took him two years to build it. It has a 102-inch wheelbase, American mags in front (without brakes), and Astro deep-dish wheels in the rear with Firestone stock car tires (with brakes in the rear). It has a stock 283-ci '57 Chevy engine with four 97 carbs atop a Weiand intake manifold. Powerglide transmission backs up to a Chevy rear end that was narrowed 10 inches. Woodgrain Formica is used on the firewall and dash, the interior is done in black Naugahyde, and the paint is yellow pearl with a rootbeer-colored frame. It was a Sweepstakes winner at the Oakland show.

Chauvin Emmons of Phoenix, Arizona, displays his bright-yellow-and-bronze hot rod at the annual Winternationals Autorama. He wanted a street roadster with all the power in the world, a hot rod that would be different, yet practical on the street. That's what he told *Car Craft* in April 1965. Chauvin built the roadster himself, getting a hand from buddy Don Robl. The wheelbase is 96 inches, and the front suspension uses a straight tube axle, torsion bars, and friction shocks. The engine is an Olds with an Engle cam, heads milled .080, ports enlarged, compression at 11.1, and Hilborn fuel injection. The transmission is from a '53 Oldsmobile with an adapter as part of the chassis. The rear end is from a '49 Olds and has been narrowed 10 inches. The interior is black Naugahyde.

Bob Mailwald of San Jose completed the work on this '32 Ford phaeton after buying it in partially finished condition. It has a '40 Ford 3-inch dropped front axle and Monroe 50/50 shocks. The steering is from a '50 Ford, and it has a column shifter and a Grant custom steering wheel. Under the louvered hood is a 265-ci '55 Chevy engine with a Duntov cam and a Rochester four-barrel. It also has a 10-inch Borg & Beck clutch, a '39 Zephyr 25-tooth gearbox, chrome wheels with '50 Mercury hubcaps, and a headlight bar with dropped ends. The upholstery is black pleated Naugahyde, and the paint is a combination of cordovan brown and '65 Mustang bronze.

I shot Darrell Pinkerton's '29 Ford on Carmel Hill between Monterey and Carmel in 1968, and in the background is Monterey Bay. Darrell had this beautiful car painted flame red, a step plate on the running board, chrome nerf bars replacing stock bumpers (front and rear), and the brake hubs redrilled to accommodate late-model Buick Riviera wheels (a common practice in the 1960s). Power came from a '56 Buick engine with an Iskenderian 3/4 cam and a four-barrel Rochester carb. The upholstery was black Naugahyde done by Banning of Gilroy.

San Jose's Greg Turretto and Herman Perez owned the radically customized "The Joker's Wild," a 1923 Model T roadster. All bodywork and paint was done by the Johnson Brothers of San Jose, and the wild nose piece holds Lucas-type lights on the bottom, parking and directional lights on top. The opening atop the nose piece shows the radiator. The chassis was made by Greg Turretto, and the front end and everything underneath is chromed. Polished magnesium wheels are fitted with Goodyear tires. The engine is a fuel-injected Ford Ardun overhead flathead. The rear end is from a Jaguar XKE and features independent rear suspension. The paint is candy cherry, and the interior, which has a full console and bucket seats, is black, wide-pleated Naugahyde. This photo was taken at the Oakland Roadster Show on February 26, 1966.

Dave Puhl of Palatine, Illinois, owned Puhl's House of Kustoms, and he came up with a new trend of asymmetrical design when he created "Illusion," a way-out yet driveable show car. I took photos of the car in 1966, a year after Illusion had been completed, when it was being shown at the Oakland Roadster Show and at the Los Angeles Winternationals Autorama. The air scoop and radiator are beneath the car, in back of the opening. The front end has completely independent suspension with Morris Minor torsion bars, trunnion-adapted Corvette spindles, adjustable heim joints, with brakes from a Corvette. Speed Headquarters, of Fox Lake, Illinois, provided the high-performance 289-ci Ford engine, and a brushed aluminum divider to the right side follows the asymmetrical layout of the car.

Dick Rundell on Long Beach, California, owned this 1928 Ford touring car, which he bought for $35 on a ranch outside Laredo, Texas. At the time he bought it, Dick said, "It had 150 bullet holes in it." He didn't care, though, because he wanted the touring badly. Cerney's Body Shop of Compton did all the body straightening and applied the candy orange paint, and Eddie Martinez did the black Naugahyde upholstery and carpets. Wire wheels are from a Buick, and it has a 301-ci Corvette engine with a Weber cam, Forgedtrue pistons, a Schiefer clutch, and Lorn fuel injectors. The injector pump and generator were mounted below the engine, and the transmission was a reworked '37 La Salle tranny, while the rear end is from a '40 Ford with a Cook quick-change. This photo was shot at the 1966 Oakland Roadster Show, where the touring won the All American Sweepstakes award.

My good friend Larry Watson painted this 1964 Ford belonging to Larry Harrison of Van Nuys, California. The color is pink pearl, with darker pink fogging lines on the hood and body contours, and the interior is black pleated Naugahyde. The Ford was extremely lowered and sported Astro chrome wheels, which were very popular. Ed Gray did all the bodywork, nosing, and decking, removing the door handles so the doors were then opened electrically. This is a good example of a mid-1960s street custom. Larry Harrison was a member of the Chancellors Car Club, and I shot this photo on February 6, 1966, at the Winternationals Autorama.

Sam Hollingsworth, or "Mr. Nomad," as he is called, hails from Palos Verdes, California, and owned this neat '57 Chevy Nomad. Sam used to race it, then he drove it on the street, and then he showed it, as seen here at the Winternationals Autorama in February 1965. Sam said it took three and a half years to finish his Nomad. Its fuel-injected engine is from a '59 Corvette, and it's a stick-shift model! Along with being lowered to the ground, the Nomad has Buick wire wheels that give it class! But most of all, Dennis Rickleffs of Rickleffs Painting Specialists of Bellflower flamed in gold pearl over candy gold, with highlighting in gold fogging. Interior work, which includes all-black pleated Naugahyde and nylon carpets, was done by Eddie Martinez.

Tony Hefner of Concord, California, showed his 1964 Buick hardtop at the 1966 Oakland Roadster Show. The extreme lowering job was done with a Hydro-electric lowering system, and the bodywork includes the hood being nosed and the trunk smoothed off. The stock grille was replaced with five chromed tubes, and there's been some custom molding of the lower body panels from the front to rear fenderwells. The wheels are polished Buick Riviera wheels with center bullets, and the interior is black Naugahyde with rolls and pleats. The paint is a candy green blended in seven shades of color, and the two trophies in front of the Buick show that it's a winner.

The 1954 America's Most Beautiful Roadster title went to Frank Rose, builder of this '27 Ford T roadster. It's seen here in the 1966 Oakland Roadster Show, at which time it was owned by John Burdick of Oakland. The roadster hadn't changed much since the mid-1950s except the front fenders were removed and a Chevy V-8 was installed. Chrysler wire wheels are used, and the aluminum rear fenders were handmade to fit the body. The front axle is a '37 Ford tube-type axle, and the steering is Ross unit while the brakes are from a '40 Ford. The three-piece hood and aluminum belly pan are by Jack Hagemann, and the black-and-white pinstriping is by Tommy the Greek. In 1971, I photographed it with owner Rebel Passalaqua for an article that appeared in the June 1971, issue of *Rod & Custom*.

At least with the Oakland Show, you had a diversity of cars. There were rods, motorcycles, sports cars, custom pickups, and customs! Here is a picture I took on February 26, 1966, of Bill Corridan's outstanding semi-custom 1961 Chevrolet hardtop coupe. The custom work was performed by the Johnson Brothers of San Jose, and included frenched dual headlights, front and rear rolled pans, an oval grille with chromed molding, and 1966 Caprice taillights. The Chevy was extremely lowered, showing off chromed Buick wire wheels. The roof has a black padded vinyl top, and the car has a 348-ci engine. The paint job was done in violet Metalflake, and it has dark-tinted windows.

This fine example of a '32 Ford roadster belonged to Ken Thornton of Sacramento, California, a member of the Thunderbirds Car Club. It took Ken two years to build the roadster, and he boxed the stock frame and used chromed '64 Corvair A-arms and coil springs, as can be seen with the front wheels turned. The rear end is from a '47 Pontiac with 3.43 gears, and the rear uses coil springs also. It has a 327-ci Chevy engine with polished heads, exhaust headers that were custom-made by Ken, and a Vertex magneto ignition. The four-barrel carb has a chromed air cleaner, and the transmission is '57 Chevy truck Hydro model. It has Buick wire wheels with UniRoyal tires. The blue cobalt firemist paint job was done by Jim Galvin, and the interior is rolled-and-pleated black Naugahyde. This photo was taken in February 1966.

Joe Kizis, producer of the Hartford, Connecticut, Auto Show had Gene Winfield build this futuristic car—the "Reactor"—to celebrate the fifteenth anniversary of his shows. Ben Delphia was the stylist of this aluminum-bodied creation, which uses a Citroen ID-19 chassis that has a low profile and offers good stability and seating over the rear axle. It has front-wheel drive, and uses a turbocharged Corvair engine with a Citroen four-speed transmission and differential unit. Splined hubs carried modified Appliance chromed wheels, and it has Firestone Indy tires and inboard disc brakes. Either electronically or by remote control, the top raises and lowers, the doors open and close, and the engine starts and accelerates. The upholstery is black Naugahyde with green metal flake inserts, and the paint is a fine Metalflake green. This picture was taken in February 1966.

Russell DeSalvo was a hot rod enthusiast in every way, as he traveled all the way from Pueblo, Colorado, with his '32 Ford three-window coupe—"Coupe To Go Go"—to enter the 1966 Oakland Roadster Show. I remember when I took this picture, I thought to myself how straight the body was, and what a beautiful black paint job this car had. The front end and everything underneath is chromed. The front axle is dropped, and the front license plate is a 1932 Colorado plate. It has a 426-ci '62 Buick engine with fuel injection and a Vertex magneto, and the chrome firewall reflection makes it look like he has two magnetos! Special bucket seats use rolled-and-pleated white Naugahyde by Sedita, and the wheels are American mags with Firestone tires.

Sacramento car builder Floyd Perry owned this 1936 Ford pickup. The top has been chopped 3 inches, the body has been sectioned 5 inches, and the rear bed has been shortened 16 inches. The front and the rear have custom-made chromed nerf bars, and the front shell and grille have 24 horizontal chrome bars. The hood is a custom-made, three-piece unit with solid side panels, and the top of the hood is fastened with Dzus fasteners. The shortened tailgate on the bed has 72 louvers, and below the tailgate is an opening with grille work that houses taillights inside. Also, the rear fenders have been bobbed. The interior is done in dark brown Naugahyde, while the bed has a dark brown tarp. Firestone "500" tires are used on polished mags. The paint is goldish-brown Metalflake, and this photo was taken at the 1966 Oakland Roadster Show.

On Saturday, June 4, 1966, the Bay Area Roadsters and the Los Angeles Roadster Club had a run to Bakersfield. Somewhere near the midpoint, the B.A.R. met up with the L.A. guys. Along the way, we usually had many stops to take short breaks, get gas, or stretch our legs. After long, hard miles in a small seating area like that of a roadster, breaks are a welcome relief. During one stop, I took this picture of Louis Bridgforth's candy Metalflake red '27 T Ford roadster. Louis did all the work himself, putting the body on a '32 frame and using a 283-ci Corvette engine and a '39 Ford transmission with a Schiefer clutch, a Ford rear end, and '47 Ford brakes. The upholstery is white Naugahyde, and it uses a combination of chrome and mag wheels with Firestone tires.

Salinas, California, 1955. Population 15,000. Even in a town this size, three shops existed: C&A (Christianson & Agostini), operating out of a ranch north of town; a service station called Breeden Bros.; and a front-end shop run by George Strobel. Richard Guess started "Goodies" in San Jose, then opened this store in April 1966, when the Salinas population was 30,000. The store was located in town at 523 S. Main St. when this picture was taken in July. It was operated by Jim Miraglia until August 1967, and Dennis Varni of San Jose operated the store afterward until closing it in 1971. The Ford roadsters parked in front are (left-right): Dick Mendonca's '29, my '29, and John Hansen's '29. All of us were Bay Area Roadster Club members.

## Chapter 4
## 1967-1969

"Rod Phaetons" made their mark on the car scene in the late-1960s, as did customs and hot rods that were more and more impressive. Construction techniques, materials, paints, plastics, and glass were being utilized in new and creative ways by car builders. Yet, as I've mentioned before, the good thing about our custom and rod builders is that the past is never completely forgotten, so enthusiastic hobbyists were building great cars in their garages along with the pros at the custom shops.

Bob Reisner's "Invader," a custom-bodied roadster, was named America's Most Beautiful Roadster at Oakland in 1967, and it scored a stunning repeat victory the following year, earning the title a second time in a tie with Joe Wilhelm's "Wild Dream," a custom aluminum roadster. In 1969, Art and Mickey Himsl won with their "Alien," a custom fiberglass roadster, and the new decade started with legendary Andy Brizio winning the 1970 honor with his "Instant T," a 1923 Ford fiberglass roadster.

Another wave of pony cars was hitting the streets in America, and the Camaro SS was the pace car at the Indianapolis 500 in 1967. The Ford Torino GT paced the race in 1968, and a Camaro SS was the pace car in 1969. Tough Texan A.J. Foyt won the 1967 Indy 500, while Bobby Unser won it in 1968, and Mario Andretti got his only victory at Indy in 1969.

Speaking of winners, the Green Bay Packers won the first two Super Bowls in 1967 and 1968, earning their place in pro football history, and actress Katherine Hepburn scored back-to-back wins as Best Actress, winning Oscars in 1967 (for "Guess Who's Coming to Dinner?") and 1968 (for "The Lion in Winter"). Newcomer Barbra Streisand (in "Funny Girl") shared the 1968 honor in a tie with Miss Hepburn.

In July of 1969, I had the pleasure of photographing Miles Foster's "Expression" '23 T bucket. Miles lived in San Carlos, California, and had Andy Brizio do the chassis work, while Archer Fiberglass made the body. Art Himsl of the Custom Paint Studio sprayed the wild mod motif with 27 different colors, and the pearl white Naugahyde upholstery was done by Mack of Sacramento. The bucket has a walnut dash with Stewart Warner gauges, and San Francisco's C & M Plating did all the chrome. It has a 301-ci '61 Chevy engine with Grant pistons, a Duntov 30-30 cam, a Cragar supercharger and manifold, and a single AFB Carburetor. Outside headers are by Sanderson. The redesigned '66 Corvette rear end has 3.70 gearing. At the 1969 Oakland Roadster Show, Miles won the Sweepstakes award in his class.

Have you heard the expression, "Ya wanna swap pink slips?" Here is an example of such a transaction taking place, shot with a tripod assist. In California, an automobile pink slip is a car's title or ownership certificate. When one sells or trades his car, he must sign his "pink slip" over to the other party. That's what Neal East and I did on Saturday, February 11, 1967, meeting each other in Buellton, midway between our homes. I traded my '29 Ford for Neal's '32 Ford. I had my roadster quite a few years and was ready for the swap, wanting to build a non-fendered '32 Ford Roadster, which can be seen on the cover of my *American Hot Rod Calendar for 1997*, published by Motorbooks International.

Al Rogers of Seattle, Washington, owned this '29 Ford roadster, the "Seven Year Itch," seen here in February 1967, at the Oakland Roadster Show. Al built the car himself, taking seven years to complete it, learning all the way through construction. The chassis is a '32 Ford, with the body channeled 9 inches over the frame and the front end out in front of the frame. The chrome front end has a tube axle and split wishbones. The radiator was lowered behind the front cross-member, and it has a chromed shell. The engine is a 1954 Dodge 241-ci engine with an Iskenderian D-800 cam, solid lifters, and adjustable push rods. Its Weiand manifold holds four 97 carbs with belled stacks, and custom outside headers have inserted mufflers. The transmission is from a '39 Ford with Lincoln gears, and the car is painted sunset orange lacquer.

At the 1967 Oakland Roadster Show, the Custom Rod of the Year award went to Joe Cruces of Vacaville for his hand-built roadster with an all-steel body, a car he called the "Crucifier." Its frame was custom-built and chrome-plated, and it had torsion bar suspension. The engine is a 283-ci Corvette with six carburetors, all backed to a Turbo transmission. The body is hinged at the rear, with the entire front lifting for easy access to the engine compartment. The nose piece has dual quad headlights, and there are air scoops on the hood and body. The grille opening runs vertically with 14 custom knobs, the truck has a custom-built bubble-type windshield, and the steering is operated by single stick in the cockpit. The paint is fuchsia Metalflake, and the interior is silver Naugahyde.

Lenny Byer of Brentwood, California, owned and operates Byer's Custom Body and Painting, and his personal roadster was a '29 Ford with a rumble seat. The paint is Metalflake purple, the interior is black Naugahyde with a diamond tuft pattern, there's a white Nylon top, and the dash panel is a modified '32 Ford with Stewart Warner gauges. The engine is from a '56 Chevy Corvette, there's a '39 Ford transmission and Lincoln gears, and the rear end is from a '40 Ford with a Halibrand quick-change center section. Engine parts and the undercarriage are completely chromed. Nineteen-fifty two Ford pickup steering is used, the front axle is dropped, and the brakes all around are from a '40 Ford. Firestone tires are mounted on polished American mag wheels. The showplace was Oakland in February 1967.

Bay Area Roadster Club member Dennis DeBenedictis of San Leandro, California, entered his '23 T roadster pickup in the 1967 Oakland Roadster Show. Under the body is a Model A frame that was narrowed and shortened to a 99-inch wheelbase, and the front has a dropped '32 axle with split wishbones—all chromed. The engine is a 327-ci 1962 Chevy with dual four-barrel carbs and a Duntov F1 cam, and custom outside headers hold mufflers inside. The transmission is from a '39 Buick, and it has a '40 Ford rear end with a Halibrand quick-change with 4.11 gears. A Moon fuel tank sits in the bed, and there's a lantern on the tailgate that serves as a taillight. The interior is black Naugahyde by George's Trim Shop in Alameda, and the paint is Omaha orange, pinstriped in black and white by the famous Tommy the Greek.

I was surprised to see this '31 Ford roadster at the 1967 Oakland Roadster Show because it was originally built in the mid-1950s by Bill Montero and his dad. The sign on the roadster said it was owned by Bob Benson but was being shown by Ron Fry. The roadster was chopped, channeled, and sectioned, and it has a three-piece aluminum hood with 138 louvers. It has a 296-ci '51 Mercury engine with an Iskenderian 1007 cam, Offenhauser heads, and dual carbs. Goodyear wide tires are on polished American mag wheels. It was originally powder blue, but at the time of this photo it had been updated with this metallic light blue, and the bucket seats are dark blue and silver Naugahyde.

"Rod Phaetons," they were called, and Reynard Moody, of Walnut Creek, California, had this one featured at the 1967 Oakland Roadster Show. Reynard constructed a tubular chassis with a chromed dropped axle and minimal springs with Moon-style brakeless front wheels. The wheelbase measured 83 inches, the '23 T body was lengthened 20 inches, it has a 327-ci Corvette engine with dual four-barrel carbs, and the transmission is a four-speed. There's a '64 Corvette chromed swing-axle rear end, and Goodyear 12.10x15-inch tires are on polished Halibrand mag wheels. Bay Area upholsterer Tony Almedo did all the black Naugahyde work, and Art Himsl painted the blue and silver Metalflake and flames.

Keith Bush had owned this 1932 Ford sedan for 10 years when I took this picture in February 1967. He bought the sedan when he was in high school in San Jose, and it was his sole means of transportation. When he got married in 1962, his wife LaJune shared his love for the family car. Their sedan is basic black with accenting that includes a copper dust beltline and white pinstriping. The interior has black Naugahyde upholstery, and the front seats are bucket-type Volkswagen seats. The front end has a dropped axle, there are '48 Lincoln brakes all around, and fancy S-shaped nerf bars replace the bumpers, front and rear. It has a 331-ci '54 Cadillac engine, and there's a '39 Ford transmission and a '32 rear end with 4.11 gears. This was the style of the times in 1967.

The oldest model to win the coveted title of America's Most Beautiful Roadster at the Oakland Roadster Show was Don Tognotti's 1914 "King T," which won the title in 1964. Here it's seen three years later and it's still in prime condition. Don started building it in July 1962 and completed it in January 1964 in his hometown of Sacramento. The front end has a hand-formed tube axle, '51 Chevy coil springs and spindles, Monroe shocks, and Airheart disc brakes. Gene Winfield did all the bodywork and the pearl "Chameleon" paint. The engine is '55 Chevy with a hydro transmission going to an independent rear suspension built by Reiff's Machine Shop. The upholstery is a pleated and button-tufted design, with chrome buttons against pearl-beige Naugahyde. Don designed the custom wheels and the new steel centers were by Reiff's.

Just before this book went to press, I talked with Carl Shrode of Burbank, California, who is 85 years *young* and still building cars, with a '27 and a '29 Ford in the works. That's great! He told me he bought this '32 Ford roadster in the mid-1960s from Bill Colgan. It had a 283-ci Chevy engine with an Isky cam and a Holley carb. The transmission was from a '39 Ford with Lincoln gears, it had a '32 Ford rear with 4.11 ratio gearing, and the brakes all around were from a '50 Mercury. Big and little tires sit on fully chromed and reversed wheels with baldy hubcaps. The bodywork and stock Chevy green paint job were done by Carl and his son Bob. The white Naugahyde upholstery and the top were done by upholsterer Bill Colgan of Burbank. This is a June 1967, photo.

On Sunday, June 18, 1967, at the Hollywood Bowl parking lot in Los Angeles, the Roadsters of L.A. presented their third roadster exhibition and swap meet. It was a fun day in the sun, and of course I took pictures. Four months prior to this event, I saw Bob Reisner at the Oakland Roadster Show, where he won the highest award, America's Most Beautiful Roadster. Bob's "Invader" *does* drive, and I saw it driving around the parking lot and even captured the moment on movie film. This concept is all Bob's idea, and includes a hand-formed aluminum body, two Pontiac GTO engines, two stick-shift hydro transmissions, and two Jaguar rear ends with disc brakes. It has fully independent front and rear suspensions, and is painted pearl with candy red, while the interior is red velvet.

The San Mateo Autorama in January 1968, is where I photographed Mike Haas's '55 Chevy Nomad wagon, which he had painted candy apple red with silver, gold, and orange. Mike, incidentally, just happens to be the son of Joe Bailon, the famous customizer and painter. The body on Mike's Nomad is strictly stock, but it was completely disassembled and restored piece by piece, with some brand new parts. The wagon has chromed lake-type pipes and a set of chromed wheels with Goodyear tires. It has a stock 283-ci Chevy engine with a pair of two-barrel carbs, and the interior is black Naugahyde. Three years after this picture was taken, the Nomad was customized once more by Mike Haas to become the "Playbunny Coach."

"Art Himsl's Mod Rod" is what this creation was called in the March 1968, issue of Rod & Custom. Shown here at the 1967 Oakland Roadster Show, this is another "Rod Phaeton," this one owned by Art Himsl of Concord. Art outdid himself with this 1916 Dodge, which was shortened 24 inches from the center, has a custom-fabricated frame, is chrome-plated, and uses a rare '33 Chrysler tube front axle with the popular-at-the-time suicide-style front end, which is brakeless. Art chose a '62 Chevy Corvette engine, a Chevy three-speed close-ratio transmission, and a '50 Oldsmobile rear with brakes. Custom headers have inserted mufflers. The interior work was done in black Naugahyde, and Art sprayed his own paint, a gold base with spectrum flames in red and green with candy orange Metalflake and glass flake for overall brilliance.

Tom Thimis, Jr., of Daly City, California, owned this '23 T roadster pickup, one of the first examples of Andy Brizio's "Instant T," which could be purchased in kit form, or you could have Andy build it for you. In this case, Tom helped Andy build the T chassis. The wheel base was 96 inches with a Pete Ogden tube front axle and Ford springs up front. The rear end is from a '56 Chevy with coil springs on top and anti-sway bars. It has a '56 Chevy 283-ci engine with a Duntov cam, an Offenhauser manifold, and an AFB carb. The headers were made by Sanderson, and Steve Archer crafted the fiberglass body. The interior is black Naugahyde. This picture was shot at the San Mateo show in January 1968.

The "Streetster" belonged to Rudy Perez of San Francisco, California, who entered his '23 T roadster in the San Mateo show in January 1968. Rudy bought a tube chassis from the Dragmaster Company in Carlsbad, and it has torsion bars, front and rear. Von Kost did the engine work on the 327-ci Chevy powerplant with Jahns pistons and a Duntov cam, and the transmission is a '57 Chevy automatic. The rear end is from a '63 Corvette with 3.30 gears. The bodywork and Metalflake gold paint are by Steve Archer, the custom outside headers are by Bogie, and the chrome-plating in front, back, and underneath is by C & M Plating. Goodyear tires sit on American mag wheels, and the pearl Naugahyde interior is by Mack of Sacramento. Rudy was a member of the Bay Area Roadster Club for many years.

At close quarters, it was very hard to find a real good angle from which to photograph this '29 Ford pickup owned Dick Durrell of Pacheco, California, at the San Mateo show in January 1968. Dick had worked on the truck for many years, fitting a '57 Chevy engine under the hood and reworking the firewall due to the engine setback. The '29 frame was boxed, the front suspension has a dropped axle, and it has '46 Ford brakes all around. The rear end is from a '57 Chevy with a Model A spring combination and handmade traction bars. The interior has red Naugahyde and black carpeting, the chromed beer keg mounted in the pickup bed holds 15 gallons of gas, and the paint is '68 Volvo Poppy red with broad gold stripes and gold fogging and pinstriping.

Bo Jones of Van Nuys, California, owned this one-of-a-kind creation. It looks like it started as a '27 T Touring, and its modified front half gives us the look of the roaring roadster days! Bo narrowed the body 8 1/2 inches and it can hold two people seated close together. The front end is a suicide-type front with long, split wishbones. The springs are quarter-elliptical and are bolted to the front axle by modified Ford perches. The headlights are early '28 Ford units, center-type steering is used, and the three-piece hood has plenty of ventilation: 290 louvers. Stuffed under the hood is a 153-ci 1962 Chevy II four-cylinder engine, the rear end is from a Model A with a Halibrand quick-change with 3.78 gears, and the wire wheels are from Kelsey Hayes. This photo was taken in June 1968.

In June 1968, the Los Angeles Roadsters' annual Father's Day Car Show and Swap Meet was held at the Great Western Exhibition Grounds in Los Angeles. One '29 Ford roadster belonged to Jeff Black of Visalia, California, a member of the Valley Roadster Club. His roadster is unusual because the body is sitting on a completely chromed '29 Ford frame. The '48 Ford rear end is chromed with a Halibrand quick-change center section, and it has a stock 1964 Chevy 327-ci engine with an Edelbrock manifold holding dual carbs. Nineteen-forty Ford spindles and brakes are used, and it has a 3-inch dropped front axle and chromed springs and wishbones.

Dick "Magoo" Megugorac of Canoga Park, California, a member of the L.A. Roadster Club, built this '29 Ford high boy roadster. He started from scratch and narrowed the '32 frame to better fit the '29 body. Notice the front bar is molded to the frame, a nice custom touch. The front axle is dropped 3 inches and is chromed, as are the springs and wishbones, shocks, brake backing plates, wheels, and hubcaps. It has a 327-ci Chevy engine with three carbs, and the transmission is an automatic, coupled to a '64 Ford rear end. A chrome fender welting divides the molded cowl from the body, and the stock windshield frame and posts are slanted back slightly. Magoo's wife Lois stitched the red Naugahyde upholstery. This shot was snapped in June 1968.

Mike Hemus, a member of the San Diego Prowlers, a well-known club of that area, owned this '27 Ford T roadster pickup. Six carbs sit atop a modified '55 340-ci Cadillac engine with a Reed camshaft with solid lifters, and milled heads with a 10.1:1 compression ratio. It has a Ford rear end a transmission from a '51 Cadillac, brakes that are '40 Fords, and chromed wire wheels with Firestone tires. Sealed-beam headlights are inside the T light housings, and the front bumper is from a Model A. The front end is chrome-plated, and has a dropped axle and split wishbones. The interior is black Naugahyde, and the beautiful black paint is accented with pinstriping, a style seen on many San Diego cars at the time, which was June 1968, when this photo was taken.

Many times during the 1960s I went to 1685 Old Mission Road, South San Francisco—the "Home Of Northern California's Instant T"—where Andy Brizio built so many of the fine show winners. From roadsters to tourings and C Cabs, they were all built here. Parked in front (at left) is Andy's red '23 "Instant T." The lad in the red jacket is Andy's son, Roy. Little did we know that years later, Brizio Street Rods would be Roy Brizio's own business. That's Andy—"The Rodfather"—in his white T-shirt walking toward his roadster. In back of Andy is Carl Mattmann's touring, with Mrs. Mattmann. This photo was shot in July 1969.

Hubby Andy Brizio built this for wife Sue in 1968. Painted a fire engine red with black flames and white pinstriping, this is one of the few "Volksrods" that were built during this era, besides Tom "Stroker" Medley's and Kent Fuller's. Power for this 1,200-pound V-Rod comes from a stock 1965 Volkswagen engine with 40 horsepower, sitting inside the '23 T pickup bed. Under the hood is modified Corvair steering, a battery, and a gas tank in the original radiator area. Mack of Sacramento did the interior with fawn tan Naugahyde. In September of 1968, Andy drove the V-Rod to a Nashville, Tennessee, rod run. Sue's friend Marilyn Miller poses for my photo.

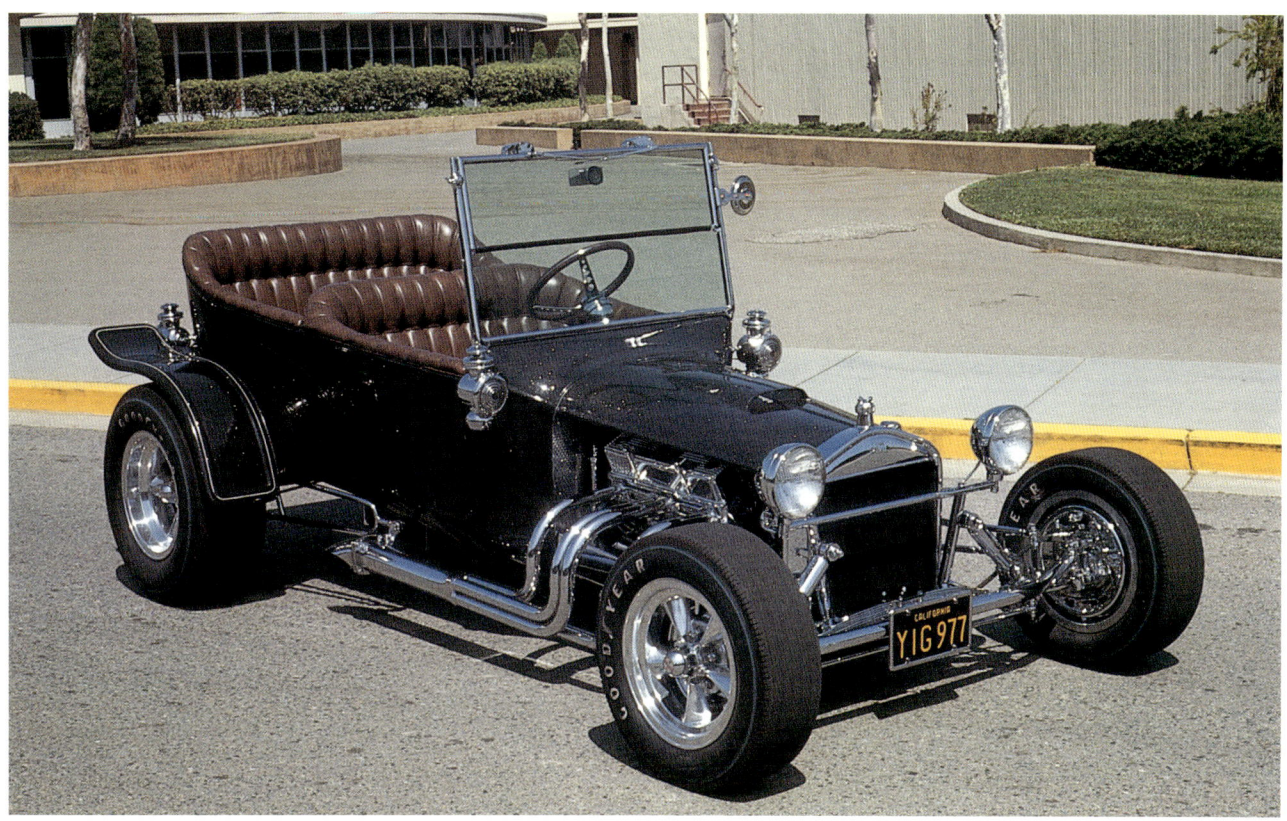

Since I presented Sue Brizio's V-Rod, I had to keep it in the family and show Andy Brizio's '23 T also. This is another outstanding example of hot rod artistry, and it won for Andy the title of America's Most Beautiful Roadster the following year, 1970. Another title went to lovely 17-year-old Kim Hobson, Miss San Bruno of 1969, who would later become Miss San Francisco. The frame is Andy's "Instant T," with a rectangular tube, a dropped 3-inch tube axle, everything chromed, and a 301-ci '57 Chevy engine with a 471 GMC Supercharger and Iskenderian 440 cam. The chromed rear end has a 3.70 ratio. Paint is American LaFrance red with Tommy the Greek black accents and white pinstriping, and it has white Naugahyde upholstery. And yes, the roadster was driven!

Carl Mattmann of Millbrae, California, owned the "C & M Special," which was special because it's the original prototype of this "Instant T" Touring model to come out of the Brizio shop in South San Francisco. Carl owns C & M Plating, which explains why everything is chromed. Andy's fiberglasser, Steve Archer, did the touring body. The frame is basically a lengthened kit-job with the wheelbase stretched out to 100 inches. It has a 327-ci '68 Chevy engine that's stock, with a single carburetor. The custom outside headers are by Sanderson of South San Francisco, and the transmission is automatic and is backed up by a chromed rear end. The dashboard is mahogany with Stewart Warner gauges, and popular at the time was the Grant steering wheel. The paint is Metalflake brown, and the brown Naugahyde upholstery was done by Mack of Sacramento.

I couldn't resist this black-and-white picture taken July 9, 1969, of Andy Brizio's '23 T on the left with 12-year-old Roy Brizio sitting behind the wheel. Roy *did* drive the roadster, and jockeyed it around into position for this photo. The model with Andy's T is Marilyn Miller. To the right is Sue Brizio, sitting in her flamed Volksrod, and next to her is Kim Hobson.

The 1969 Oakland Roadster Show winner was the custom-bodied "Alien" by Art (left) and Mickey Himsl.

# Index

"Ala Kart", 87
"Alien", 23, 109, 127
"Astro", 34
"Avenger", 15
"Coupe To Go Go", 104
"El Matador", 28, 34
"El Tangerino", 39, 40
"Emperor", 9, 23
"Expression", 109
"Futurista", 52
"Ghost", 23, 69
"Illusion", 93
"Instant T", 23, 109, 118, 124
"Invader", 23, 109, 116
"Iron Indian", 78
"Jade Idol", 26
"King T", 115
"Mark Mist", 25
"Mystique", 86
"Pointless", 81
"Predicta", 24
"Reactor", 103
"Seven Year Itch", 110
"Sharkamino", 61
"Solar Scene", 53
"Streetster", 119
"The Astro", 59
"The Beatnik Bandit", 25
"The Copper Cart", 77
"The Joker's Wild", 93
"The Mantaray", 89
"The Moonshiner", 43
"The Seaburst", 72
"Twister T", 9, 23
"Wild Dream", 23, 109
"XR-6", 23, 54
Alexander, Mike, 48
Almedo, Tony, 113
America's Most Beautiful Roadster, 20, 39, 54, 69, 71, 100 109, 115, 116
Anderson, Bud, 48
Archer, Steve, 118, 119, 125
Bailon, Joe, 27, 79, 117
Banning, 47, 59, 73, 92
Barrett, Lee, 34, 71, 81
Barris Kustoms, 24, 54, 71
Barris, George, 9, 23, 46, 50, 55, 61, 86
Barris-Geraghty, 16
Bay Area Roadster Club, 7, 32, 37, 65, 69, 74, 75, 81, 83, 107, 112, 119
Bell, Fred, 84
Benson, Bob, 112
Besser, Jack, 52
Biro, Pete, 50
Black, Jeff, 121
Bottie, Joe, 63
Boucher, Gene, 31
Bridgfourth, Louis, 106
Brizio, Andy, 23, 109, 118, 124, 126
Brown, Tut, 65
Buchan, John, 21
Burdick, John, 100
Burgos, Vince, 72
Burke, Bill, 75
Burrell, Jim, 89
Byer, Lenny, 111
C & M Plating, 109, 119, 125
C & M Special, 125
Calvert, Gary, 86
*Car Craft* Dream Rod, 56, 57
Cardoza, Tony, 28, 29
Casper, Carl, 23, 69
Chancellors Car Club, 78, 95
Chrisman, Art, 16

Cushenbery, Bill, 59
Clark, Jim 39, 69
Clenendon, Bill, 72
Clifford, Gil, 27
Colgan, Bill, 116
Collins, Riley, 21
Conway, Hershel, "Junior", 24, 55, 74
Corp, Terry, 66
Corpora, Jasper, 12
Corral, Gary and Ken, 86
Corridan, Bill, 101
Cosma Ray, 70
Costa, Harry, 25
Curtin, Robert, 19
Cushenbery Custom Shop, 28, 31, 48
Cushenbery, Bill, 7, 23, 34, 41, 48, 50, 51, 56
Darren, James, 61
Dean, Dick, 75
Del Curto, Dick, 27
Delphia, Ben, 103
DeSalvo, Russell, 104
Dobeckmun Co., 85
Dreyer, Alex, 74
Durrell, Dick, 119
East, Neal, 110
Emmons, Chauvin, 90
Emory, Neil, 60
Fernandes, Mel, 19
Fernandez, John, 59
Flint, Dick, 82
Ford, Eddie, 87
Foster, Miles, 109
Freedlun, Warren, 34, 69
Fry, Ron, 112
Fuller, Kent, 124
Galvin, Jim, 102
Golden State T, 83
Goular, Ray, 79
Goulart, Raymond, 76
Grabowski, Norm, 9, 34, 36
Gray, Ed, 95
Greenwade, Bob, 70
Gregg, Beverly, 60
Guasco, Rich, 9, 23
Guess, Richard, 107
Haas, Mike, 117
Hagemann, Jack, 100
Hannon, Paul, 32, 65
Hansen, John, 69, 107
Harrison, Larry, 95
Hefner, Tony, 98
Heliker, Gary, 9
Hemus, Mike, 123
Henderson, Hugh, 15
Henning, Joe "Guiseppe", 25
Hentzell, Don, 32
Heredia, Rudy, 11, 47, 71
Hill, Steve, 55
Hill, George, 76
Hill, Graham, 69
Himsl, Art and Mickey, 23, 43, 109, 127
Himsl, Art, 109, 113, 117
Hines, Bill, 58
Hollingsworth, Sam, 97
Holmes, John, 64
Homen, Eddie, 23
House Of Color, 55
House Of Wheels, 61
Huff, Ed, 71, 81
Jackson, Dick, 48
Jeffries, Dean, 7, 72, 89
Jensen, Clayton, 60
Joe Bailon Customs, 39

Joe Ortiz's Custom Shop, 20
Johnson, Bud, 10
Jones, Bo, 121
Jue, Lee, 72
Kaegle, Bill, 84
Kaline, Walt, 50, 74
Kemmerer, LeRoy, 26
King, Allen, 77
Kinnard, Jo Dee, 83
Kizis, Joe, 103
Kofoed, Duane, 82
Kost, Von, 119
Kraus, Bob, 84
Krikorian, Chuck, 9, 23
Kugie's Kar, 37
Kugler, Don, 37, 71
Larivee, Bob, 56
Lee, Gary, 74
Lokey, Don, 23, 69, 71
Lorero, Don, 79
Los Angeles Roadster Club, 7, 9, 34, 50, 52, 66, 106, 122
Lustre Chrome Plating, 50, 74
Lykken, Steve, 90
M&M Muffler Shop, 11
Mack, 109, 119, 124, 125
Madame FeFe, 21
Mailwald, Bob, 90
Manger, Bill, 23, 29, 34, 41, 57, 59
Marasco, Dave, 32, 71, 75
Marasco, Fred, 73, 74
Marquis, 31
Marshall, Bill, 81, 85
Martinez, Eddie, 10, 25, 55, 58, 87, 94, 97
Mathews, Don, 31
Mathews, Ray, 23
Mattmann, Carl, 124, 125
Mayfield, Bob, 20
McDaniels, Joe, 29
McKay, Jack, 74
McMullen, Tom, 36
McNulty, Bob, 61
Medley, Tom, 124
Megugorac, Dick, 122
Mendonca, Dick, 25, 32, 71, 107
Millard, Bud, 31
Miller, Charles, 81
Miller, Mox, 48
Miraglia, Jim, 83, 107
Monterey Kar Kapades, 7, 11, 20, 24, 28, 32, 61, 63
Montero, Bill, 112
Moody, Reynard, 113
Munson, George, 87
Nancy, Tony, 54
National Custom Auto Fair, 70
Neumann, Bill, 50, 51
Oakland Roadster Show, 7, 9, 13, 15, 16, 19, 21, 27, 28, 39, 44, 46, 47, 50, 51, 60, 61, 69, 79, 81, 89, 93, 94, 98, 100, 104, 105, 109-113, 115-117, 127
Ogden, Pete, 118
Paris Auto Show, 51
Passalaqua, Rebel, 100
Paulsen, Pete, 61
Pere, Patria, 70
Perez, Herman, 93
Perez, Rudy, 52, 119
Perry, Floyd, 105
Pinkerton, Darrell, 92
Powell, Rod, 80, 86
Price, Ron, 13

Puhl, Dave, 93
Randall, Robert, 26
Rathman, Jim 9
Reiff's Machine Shop, 115
Reinero, Dennis, 18
Reisner, Bob, 23, 109, 116
Reynolds Aluminum Special, 75
Richards, Pinky, 58
Rickleffs, Dennis, 48, 97
Road Knights, 11
Roadia, Al, 83
Robl, Rob, 90
Rogers, Al, 110
Rose, Frank, 100
Roth, Ed, 25, 50
Rundell, Dick, 94
Sacramento Autorama, 18, 20
Sahagon, Jerry, 13, 20
San Diego Prowlers, 123
San Jose Autorama, 7, 10, 12, 14, 27, 33, 47, 70, 71
San Jose Roadster Club, 72
San Mateo Autorama, 25, 26, 31, 41, 43, 44, 46, 51, 87, 117
Sanderson, 109, 118, 125
Sanford, Larry, 60
Sawyer, Buzz, 11
Scoopie Doo, 28
Scritchfield, Dick, 66, 84, 87
Sharp, Greg, 75
Sharp, Lore, 27
Shrode, Carl, 116
Silhouette, 34, 41, 51
Silva, Ray, 32
Slonaker, Al, 19, 51
Smith, LeRoi "Tex", 23, 34, 39, 54
Solimine, George, 52
Specht, Don, 83
Star Custom Show Cars, 52
Starbird, Darryl, 24, 50, 52, 70
Stefan, Gordon, 28
Strobel, George, 107
Strutz, Glenn, 83
Swaja, Steve, 54
Taormino, Mel, 33, 49
Thimis, Jr., Tom, 118
Thornton, Ken, 102
Thunderbirds Car Club, 102
Tocchini, Joe, 39
Tognotti, Don, 15, 23, 39, 115
Tommy the Greek, 52, 63, 100, 112
Torres, Rudy, 14
Turretto, Greg, 92
Valley Roadster Club, 121
Varner, Don, 41
Varni, Dennis, 107
Vido, Doug, 78
Villa Riviera, 61
Ward, Rodger, 9
Watson, Larry, 7, 12, 20, 58, 78, 95
Waymier, Dutch, 86
Wells, Lee, 46, 74
Wheelers Club, 12
Wilde, Willie, 86
Wilhelm Custom Shop, 25, 49
Wilhelm, Joe, 23, 25, 50, 51, 59, 109
Winfield's Custom Shop, 18, 26
Winfield, Gene, 7, 26, 44, 45, 50, 53, 54, 103, 115
Winternationals Autorama, 90, 93, 95, 97
Winternationals Car Show, 48, 49, 53, 55, 58-60, 71, 74, 75, 78, 89
XMSC, 16
Zocchi, Richard, 44, 45